Someone Almost Loved Me to Death

Part II
"The Silent Screams Series"

Book design by: Ronika Hughes with
Ambri'ance Graphic Design
ambriancedesign@gmail.com

Someone Almost Loved Me to Death

Yolanda Lee-George

While the publisher has made every attempt to release correct addresses and contact information at the time of this publication, the publisher assumes no responsibility for errors or changes that come about after the publish date.

Black~Butterfly Publishing Inc.
www.bethanysgroup.com
yolanda@bethanysgroup.com

Please help in the fight against piracy of Copyrighted materials. Purchase only authorized editions.

ISBN: 978-0-9910760-0-0
© 2013 Black~Butterfly Publishing Inc.
New Addition

AUTOGRAPH
PAGE

To My Best Friend and God~Sister

Yolanda, of 26 years, I would like to congratulate you on your recent success of completing your books. I have personally been there to witness your recurrent struggle with domestic violence. Throughout this time I have observed your ex-husband, take out his unstable battle of rage on you. I must say through it all you have remained strong for yourself and for your kids. You have held your head high as a single mother of 5 and grandmother of 3. You are a courageous individual and it has been days when you were on the run even when you had to run to my house. I was there for the birth of several of your kids, but also saw the short lived joyous occasion end due to tragic effects of domestic abuse that took place right after. I recall one specific time when you had just given birth and he beat you outside in the yard, then wet you with a water hose. I had never in my life witnessed such a thing as to what I saw that day. That was something that I can just still close my eyes and see. Yet, you held your head high and said, "Brina, let's go", as though nothing happened. I will never forget that day. There have been many other incidences and I could go on, but you went through several days like that where you just kept it moving. Another time I can recall; days that you were on the run and he couldn't find you. Some of those days were just as bad as the days he would hit you because the things that he would say and refer to you as, wasn't acceptable even to an animal, but still you held your head high.   As I mentioned I could continue with stories and painful memories, but I am grateful and can only thank God that you and your kids came out this abuse alive.   In closing, I would like to say "look what God has done and look where he has brought you and your kids from 'until this day."   I love you and the kids and always will. God have kept us in each other's lives for a reason. We have been sisters, friends and most of all each other's strength. Thank you Lord for our togetherness and friendship.

Love you always,

Sabrina Chandler

Heart of Hope Award Acknowledgment
By Attorney Rosemary Armstrong:

As a volunteer lawyer I have worked with many victims of domestic violence. As a young teen I cowered as I watched it happen in my own home. I know how abusers rob their victims of the ability to make good choices. The winner of our first annual Heart of Hope Award was the victim of unspeakable abuse for over ten years, and her abuser was her own husband. She called herself "a puppet on a string" because of the control he exerted over her.   But through her faith she found the courage, determination, and strength to break out of the shackles he had imposed and to leave him. The leaving was not easy because she had 5 young children to take with her. Yes, it was faith that made her leave, but as my mother always told me "God helps those who help themselves" and our winner helped herself mightily by retaining Bay Area Legal Services to represent her. She got her life back and is currently an employee of the Hillsborough County Bar Association and a Bay Area Legal Services board member. We often describe the acts of people who overcome adversity and turn their lives around as "making lemonade out of lemons." Today's winner of the Heart of Hope Award not only made lemonade out of lemons, she opened a lemonade stand. She speaks publicly on behalf of Bay Area Legal Services and created

Bethany's Group, a faith based organization whose mission is to help and encourage families to overcome abuse and to become more self-reliant.

Of our winner, our colleague Margaret Mathews has said: She has given such a great gift to our community by sharing her story which demonstrates how her pain has transformed into strength and hope for herself and her children. Dick Woltmann, the Executive Director of Bay Area Legal Services, also praises our winner: She has talked about her experience as a victim of domestic violence to numerous groups that have included some of the most powerful and respected people in Tampa. She accurately conveys the horror of the violence, but also conveys the positive life that is possible for those who survive. The plaque for our winner states that it is "in recognition for transforming her life through courage, determination, and dedication to helping others. Yolanda achieved a personal victory over difficult circumstances, enabled herself and her family to break the cycle of domestic violence, and empowered others to take action." The winner of our first annual Heart of Hope Award is *Yolanda Lee.*

Acknowledgements

Bay Area Legal Service for all that you have done for me, I don't know where I would be without your services. *Beth* you have been such an inspiration in my life, you've loved me, supported me, encouraged me and your kind words help to build my self-esteem; because of the love that you showered me with and the support you pushed into me, my group is named after you "Bethany's Group" Thank you for loving me genuinely. *Dick, Sally, Judy* and so many others there at BALS have been such an inspiration in my life and for that I'm grateful. *Rosemary A.*, for always supporting me in everything I do and sharing so much of your personal self with me, THANK YOU!

Pastor & Sister Daniel (Cyvonne) Davy, thank you for being my spiritual dad and mom at *New Life Tabernacle U.P.C.* (of Tampa, FL), your love alone kept me drawn closer to the love of God, Thank you so much dad and momma Davy, I've been a part of the NLT family for 16 years and I'm still standing through my ups and downs and you've loved me even still. To the rest of my New Life family that cried, worshipped, fast, prayed and was an ear to me, *Mother Gooden (S.I.P mommy), Sis. Tracy, Sis. J.R., Sis. Dionne, Sis. Terrica, Sis. Ferguson* and some of the others that quietly knew of my pains…THANK YOU for loving me during these times. I loved you yesterday and I'll love you ladies till death. Thank you (my now Pastor) *Pastor Rashidi Collins* for always speaking a word into my spirit and I know eyes have not seen and ears have not heard what God has in store…I love you *Pastor Collins* and *First Lady Sis. Collins* of **Victory Tabernacle U.P.C.** *Vondalyn "Fuggie" Bryant, Georgette Gunn and Felecia "Cookie" Lee* thanks for allowing the kids and me to take refuge at your homes, I Love you so much!

Special Thanks

Lorenzo George, Sr, my now handsome husband, who held it down for me while I stressed to revise and update my books, thank you for being my hide-a-way, allowing me to hide in your arms when the rest of the world seemed to be moving in a world wind, I love you Mr. George. *Leon and Sabrina Chandler*…I love you both so much words can't even begin to explain or say what roles you've played in my life even now. You were our shelter from the storm so many nights and I don't know what we would have done without you. I don't even have to say much about you two, the love and appreciation is so embedded in my heart! WE LOVE YOU SO MUCH! Thank you to Rick and Kena Hummel (George F. Young, Inc) for your love and support through all of this madness, although I worked for you, you both were my work "Me'maw and Paw" and I love you both so much! **Dwayne Sanders** WOW, thank you for turning my real life story into an

AWESOME stage play **"He Apologized"**, you're the best! Love you!

My ex-husband for taking me through pure hell, but God made my enemy my footstool *Psalm 110:1 The LORD says to my Lord: "Sit at my right hand until I make your enemies a footstool for your feet."* What I went through with you gave me the strength to be who I am today, I'm strong, I'm a beautiful BLACK woman, I'm healthy, I'm a Royal Priest Hood, I'm Chosen by the hand of the Master who is Jesus Christ and NO ONE can ever take that from me again, I have a testimony about the test I endured by your hands, I don't hate you, I love you and pray for you. What the devil set up to be bad, God turned it around for my good. May God cover you under His blood!

To My Children: Nijah Jonte'e, Johnna, Johntavia, Johnavia, John III

Wow, I love you guys so much, we made it out, and we are safe, we are covered under the blood of Jesus, no weapon that was formed against us was able to prosper. God did a new thing in us and all though we go through and we still have some battle scars, it just shows that we made it through the war. I want to apologize for the prison I held you all captive in for all those years, but I'm grateful that although it was hell, God held us in the palm of His hands and we never gave up. I'm proud of all of you and I love you all so much. **Nijah** my oldest baby, I thank God you where shielded from the most of it (although you saw enough), I'm grateful for the man you are today, you are an awesome son, you are an awesome outstanding father and I love you; **Johntavia**, it's been a bumpy road, but God is not through with you yet. God didn't bless you with that voice to sing for nothing, HE didn't give you the gift of the Holy Ghost speaking in tongues to just waste, God has HIS time set for you too baby, what you're doing now is going to be your "Silent Screams" testimony... that God will be glorified, just hold on baby, it's coming. God said in *Acts 2:39 For the promise is unto you, and to your children, and to all that are afar off, even as many as the Lord our God shall call*. I receive that in the name of Jesus! **Johnavia**, you were just a baby and don't remember much, but you did remember calling him the monster, I'm glad to see that you have grown past that hurt and anger and that God has matured you and you are such a beautiful black baby doll to me. I love you and I know God has His hands all around you. You are my professional baby. **John III**, although you carry the name and so much anger because even as a baby you still remember some things; but don't dwell on that, you're my athletic baby and God has you right where He wants you, with you I have to continue to call those things that are not as though there were because the devil keeps trying to take you in the genetic direction OH BUT GOD... I'm a praying woman and the enemy can't have my baby. Continue to be strong in the Lord and know that you are not validated or justified by your name or your title, but your actions. You are a praying young man, so be that young man that prayed and knows how to call on the name of Jesus. I love you baby. **Johnna**, I kept you last for a reason (although you're the second oldest child) my GOD my baby, my strength, my safety zone through God...Baby, as I sit and type this brief but important part to you, I sit here with tears rolling down my face at work. Johnna I don't know how I would have done this without you, baby you were my strength, my prayer partner, my survival kit. Your childhood was snuffed from under you in the blank of an eye all because of the man you call the monster. I was so busy trying to fill a void, be validated, be strong and prove to the person that belittled me as a child, that I was capable of having someone to love me. I was seeking something that only God was able to give me but I didn't know how to go about it. God blessed you with the gift of the Holy Ghost speaking in tongues at the young age of 8 years old, God is a God that don't make mistakes because we prayed together, we did spiritual warfare together, we even fast together, you've even anointed me, the other kids and yourself. You were a child but you never left my side. You are a beautiful strong woman, mother, daughter and sister and I love you more than you can ever imagine. Even today our bond is one that some can't seem to understand. *Johnna Nytajah Lee*, you are my star baby and I know God is going to allow you to shine because you're about to step OUT of your **"Silent Screams"** and I won't leave your side! I love you baby forever.

Where I am today! I want to thank you Lord for keeping me in the eye of the storm, shielding and protecting me from death. Today I'm stronger, wiser and much better and it's all by your grace and mercies. I work full-time for the Hillsborough County Bar Association, I sit on the Board of Directors for Bay Area Legal Service, I've started my own support group "Bethany's Group" for families in abuse (of any kind), I'm a motivational speaker, I'm a grandmother and now I'm an Author, but most of all I'm Alive! Thank you Jesus for loving me. **I SHALL NOT BE MOVED**…stay tuned…

Introduction from Author

I'm sure those of you that read my first book, *"Someone To Love The Little Girl In Me"* are trying to figure out how in the world a woman who was so cold emotionally on the inside, could end up being an abused woman, struggling to break away not only physically, but emotionally from her abuser. Sometimes even the coldest heart can be won over with a little warmth, and sometimes even with all the running around, the wild acts, and the pretending, you know that deep down inside of you, there is that part that just wants to be loved by someone. It's that person that you feel can fill that void in your life. I can't fully express to you what happened, all I can say is that inside of this bad girl, there was a little girl that only wanted to be loved and nurtured. Some people tend to judge you before they know you, and if you read part one of this series, you have a picture, but it has not totally been developed yet. Some of the choices that I made in my life were due to much of the hurt I endured growing up. I've always wanted someone to love me for whom I was, and not for who they thought or wanted me to be. I've always tried to medicate my pain by putting a different kind of bandage on it, and never actually allowed my healer "Jehovah Rapha" to completely heal this pain within me. For so long I've put a bandage over my hurt and in other words, I put a bandage on a painful sore, that I didn't even clean out first, a sore that I just covered up with all the filth, all the yucky stuff that needed some medicine, some treatment, then it begins to stink, it begin to run ooze would show through the bandage and it was slowly decaying but I never paid it any attention INTENTIONALLY. I'd eventually take the bandage off because it had grown a scab. As life goes on you may tend to bump the area of the sore and the pain reminds you that something is hurting underneath, something is still there unhealed and sometimes you hit it hard enough it will tear the scab away and it begins to bleed or ooze, and you can now see it decaying underneath. That's what I did to my life, I allowed the pain from my upbringing to decay and didn't allow my Jesus to heal that what was in me and even today I've not fully allowed God to completely make me whole. I know God is working it out for my good, so **"Yes I Trust You Lord".**

Now this is the continuation of my healing because God is in the healing business, I pray after this book is published, that I will have gone through an even greater healing. I will have found more self-esteem and doing more of the will of God. Amen. I wanted someone to love me but instead, *Someone Almost Loved Me to Death!* I was always told that "What goes on in the house, stays in the house!" Well I did that, but what they didn't tell me was that the house is usually on fire and no one on the outside sees it because you're windows are closed, even if they see or smell smoke, if no one is screaming, people will only walk by and assume. You can keep the secrets confined within the walls, but they then become your jailers, and you have arrested and secretly sentenced your spirit to house arrest or solitary confinement without having the chance to be free. It's time to be released from the prison that the enemy has tried to hold me in for so many years' **TIME SERVED**!

As you read this information, it may appear that I'm jumping from place to place (and I am) because I'm telling my real life and as I begin to type, I remember different things and will drop it in as I go. This is just my story to let you know that God is able to do just what HE said HE would do; this is my story to let you know that "you don't have to die in the abuse", that **"THERE IS LIFE AFTER THE ABUSE"**. To get out and trust in God for your safety AMEN! HERE WE GO!

Table of Contents

Table of Contents

This is the last chapter from the first book in the Series titled *"Someone To Love The Little Girl In Me"*

Chapter 29 – Same Ole Games Man, Come On

Things were beginning to feel like I was stuck in a bad episode of my favorite show. I enjoyed certain parts of my life, they were exciting, but then other parts were still stuck in that rut. If you can imagine having your favorite meal on the table before you, but with it, you have old and dirty silverware, and the plates are nasty. You want the food, but the extra stuff just kills the excitement, and so you can't focus on how much you want that meal because of what you would have to go through to get it. I mean John was still up to his usual stuff, after all of those years. He was still trying to sleep with as many women as he could. At some point you would think that a man would grow up, and start thinking with his other head, but not this one, he was going to be a dog until he died. I wasn't feeling him anymore like I use to, I had already made the move to be by myself once before, but this time it was different. I needed to move forward and find out what was out there for me. I wanted to raise my kids, and keep it moving. So John and I officially broke up for real. This was not like all of the other times, when it was breaking off; we were really breaking up and letting it all go. I wanted to allow all the women who he wanted to sleep with, to have him. So I put his stuff out and he came by with his cousin, and they got everything out of the front yard. I locked my door and let them load the truck and it was a wrap. John and I went our separate ways, and it was hard at first because it was just the company that I was missing, I wasn't missing the man anymore because he hadn't played that roll in a while.

Now I can't take it away from him that he was always been a hard worker, he was just making crazy decisions, and he wanted every woman in the world. It was tired of watching him get diseases and in my mind I figured that it would be AIDS next, and I wasn't trying to have that so I got out of that line of fire. I also didn't catch any more diseases because I was no longer sleeping with him. You would think that going through all of this would be enough to be the entire story, but this was only the beginning!

Chapter 1 – Meeting My Monster!

I was still living in the duplex by the interstate as I continued to hustle and dance a little while longer. I used to hang out with my cousin every now and then and we would go riding around town sometimes to see what was going on. She was dating one of John's friends named, Darren, and we would get their cars to just ride and wild out with them. Every now and then we would go through College Hill (Jackson Height) and we would run into this guy. I knew him when I was younger because my aunt lived over in Jackson Height but I never paid him any attention. He also remembered seeing me dance in the club. He knew that I was a woman that didn't take any mess off of any man. He knew that I was a woman about my money, my business and I hustled by any means necessary. He claimed that he was attracted to me because of my demeanor. We would talk to him every time we saw him, and he would always try to give me the eye but I didn't pay him any attention.   He didn't care that I was going out with John when he tried to approach me. He always called me by the nickname Black but I was still too busy playing mind games with men. I knew no one would ever actually love me, so as they played games, so did I. (Secretly I did wish someone would come into my life and truly love me. I wanted to feel what love was. I only had an idea of what it felt like, being as I never had or saw it growing up) the only love I had was from my dad but that was different.

When me and my god-sister GG used to hang out, we would sometimes run into him and he'd try to get me to go with him but I refused although I would tease him. A few times we'd see him out at the club and I would promise to meet up with him or tell him I was coming back to see him, but I never did. I did that for quite a while, even to the point of taking him to a hotel room, getting the room and telling him I'd be back but never came back. I never felt like it would turn into anything, even though I wasn't looking because I was with someone already and he and I was both playing each other. He was very attractive and I liked his little swag, but still it was nothing. I saw him as one of my little preys, someone to tease but yet I was still hesitant when it came to him for some strange reason.

A few months of still running into him teasing him but never connecting with him, John and I departed our ways, so I was really having fun now (as if I wasn't already).

One day when riding through College Hill, I saw him walking and asked GG to pull next to him so I could bother him. When we pulled up beside him, I asked him if I could walk with him or give him a ride. (I had no real intentions of giving him a ride, just bothering him as usual). He said he was going to his mom's house, so we gave him a ride. As the drive went on he began to ask me when I was going to give him a date. I responded with a simple "soon." He asked if he saw me at the club later that night, if I would consider going off with him for real this time. I teased him as usual and told him that I would take him to my house. He asked if he could stay all night and I told him, only if he's worth keeping all night. He assured me that he would definitely be spending the night and we shook on it. As we drove off, GG and I laughed because we both knew that I had just run another line on him, another one of my games, and that I wasn't really going to see him.

Later that night – back in College Hill, I ran into him again and tried to hide but he walked up on me too fast. (I was actually seeing another dude in College Hill and that's why I was trying to hide). I was determined not to go off with him by myself, so I told GG that she better not leave me because I wasn't going off with him by myself. So when he asked if he could go with us, we told him that he would have to try and get GG's friend out of the house in order for all of us to hang out. He went and got her friend out of the house so we could go to a movie and to eat. GG and I decided we didn't want to go to the movies and planned to get rid of them as fast as we could so we could make it to the club and I can see my other friend. We all went back to my place for a little while, and ended up having a lot of fun. It got late so GG decided to spend the night with me, but she had to leave to take her friend home leaving me and him there and we really had a nice time together.

Chapter 2 – Sleeping With the Enemy

He really portrayed the image of being a really nice guy. Of course we ended up in bed and I must say he had a lot of confidence in himself because he also ended up spending the night. In all honesty, the man was 100% and some in bed. I noticed that he snorted cocaine all night though and even offered me some, but I turned him down and told him I didn't use that stuff. I sold cocaine but I didn't say anything because I had my thing with snorting and didn't get hooked so who am I to judge (Even if I was still snorting, I never let any guy, especial that I was messing with/sleeping with, know that I snorted or did anything other than drink).   He was at my house back and forth for 2 weeks straight after that night and everything seemed to be perfect. He didn't want to leave, but he had to because I was a hustler and I didn't stick with one man too long (just wasn't ready for it after John) and outside of that, he was a hustler as well. Yet again, I noticed he snorted heavy every night and I had even given him a sack of mine every now and then but I didn't think anything of it, boy was I totally wrong.

I took him to get a change of clothes throughout that week to what I thought was his cousins' house. The entire time it was actually the house of another woman that he'd been dating. Since she knew he was a dealer, she assumed that most of the time he was out grinding all night (selling his drugs). He was playing her for a fool as well because he was with me for 2 full weeks and he didn't even get a chance to hustle. It came to the point where he needed to make some money because my money was a continued flow his money wasn't. He did finally leave one morning to go and do his thing but to my surprise he came back that night and stayed. I noticed he seemed to be intimidated by some of the things that I had going on in my life. I have always been very independent and didn't count on anyone to do things for me. I always had a nice place of my own and transportation. I did what I had to do for myself and didn't bother other people about doing anything for me. Being as though I was hustling, I had a lot of male friends and I knew a lot of dealers that would come by to kick it with me. Being as he wasn't my man, I still had personal friends stopping by to see me as well. Then he felt like he didn't have to call before he came by and that he could just come over when he wanted to. I wasn't looking for a relationship with him because the dude didn't have a car or really anything to bring to my table. I didn't need less or equal, I needed a plus. He would make his little comments about the fact that I was hustling and he really didn't want me doing it. He didn't want me modeling anymore either, he just wanted all of my undivided attention but

I couldn't give that to him because I was about my business. It slowly got to the point where he wanted to know my every move. When clients came by to pick up a package (drugs of course), he'd go to the door with me just to see what they were saying and to make sure that the next man saw him. It was a little crazy but me being me; I was saying silly shit in my head like "I guess I put it on this dude because he is in my ass every second" I blew it off SILLY ME. **HAS ANYONE NOTICED SOME EARLY WARNING SIGNS YET?** I continued to do my thing, and didn't care if he did his. I wasn't looking for a relationship, as I have been so adamantly stating, I was just hanging out and pretty much being content in my life as I was worn out with believing someone would come into my life, be faithful and love me. I simply wanted to just be free to be me and do as I pleased.

Chapter 3 – Overlooking Warning Signs

He got to where he wanted to know where I was going and who I was going with. He didn't want me to wear lips stick or lip gloss when I went out anymore because it made my lips look inviting (as he said). He really didn't want me to wear high heeled shoes when I left the house because he said I walked provocative. At this point I wore heels just in the house for no reason because I loved wearing my heels! Hell I'd run track or play basketball in my heels. Brina is a witness to how he would act about the heels and lipstick/lip gloss, but these are the things that also attracted him to me. **WARNING SIGN**

We used to go get ice cream cones from McDonald's all the time because my daughter loved them, but he got to the point that he didn't't' want me to even eat a damn ice cream cone out in public because he said men watch the way that I eat the ice cream off the cone. When we first got together, he realized that I was just as well-known as he was and he used that to his advantage. He wanted to be seen everywhere with me, but I wasn't feeling all of that. He wanted me to continue to look good at first but once he messed around and got into me, he slowly started the jealous foolishness. I had pictures all over my house of my family, the kids with their father and just pictures of my life. He was even intimidated by the pictures, saying that I must be keeping them around for memories of my ex's. I told him that I kept pictures because I like to take pictures and so my kids will have their memories for when they got older. Still I really wasn't paying him too much attention because what he was talking about meant nothing to me. For me, it was a sex thing. Eventually he went behind my back and threw all of my pictures away. I found them outside in the trash and my neighbor Patrice had gotten them and hid them in her house.

I started to realize he wasn't hanging out as much as he did at first. I also noticed that he was snorting even more cocaine.

While just sitting around the house chilling, he would trip a little more when he was on powder and say things like "Who was that" for no apparent reason. I'd laugh because I thought he was joking. He knew damn well there wasn't anyone in the house, so he had to be joking. He would ask me if I was with someone, and why do my lips look like they are moving, all that kind of foolish stuff, but again, I ignored him. I thought he was joking. I had never met anyone that actually hallucinated so I didn't think twice about it. **WARNING SIGN** One time we were playing and he busted my lip by mistake (or was it). I said, "Man you burst my lip now people are going to think you jumped on me," he said, "That ain't all I'll do to your ass, they better know I'll kick your ass." We both laughed and kept it moving not taking it serious.

After it had been well over a month or so (that we'd been seeing each other) I realized he was under me so much I had not really been doing any dancing or modeling (because every now and then I would still go and do both). My daughter had begun to like him (she had just turned three years old). He used to take her to buy pickles, cheddar cheese, chips with dip then he would sit with her and let her just do what she wanted to do. To me he was really good with her and I normally did not let a man around my children, especially my daughter. He literally played with her all the time. He was a very playful person and we would even have water balloon fights in the house. We would play wrestle and tease about certain things and just play. When I'd tease him about me being with another man and he would tell me that he would kill me before he let another man get me. Some things we would play about, he'd tell me that he would knock me out, but I didn't take it to heart. We played around like that. "Silly me."

WARNING SIGN

Chapter 4 – My Comfort Zones

I finally started getting comfortable with him, to a place where I would lie in his arms and tell him about my childhood. How I felt my mom never loved me, and that she cherished my sister over me. I told him how the only love I had ever felt was from my dad. He was always so attentive. He'd let me lay in his lap, he'd kiss me, rub me and seemed to take care of me (and it felt so good). It wasn't just sex with us anymore. I felt he was there with and for me. I didn't realize while laying in his arms where I felt safe, telling him all my hurts, dreams and desires, that he would recording it in his brain to turn around and use it against me. He would run my bath water, sit on the tub and bathe me, stand there to dry me off, lotion my body completely, and oiled me down. It felt good to have that attention, but of course I did all of the same things to him plus more. I had not been hanging around with GG as much (or anyone for that matter) because he was under me so much (Never realizing he was forming my life into abuse and didn't even see it right under my nose). Being as my car was messed up, I used to get a way to wash clothes, grocery shop and do whatever it was that I needed to do. I always got around with no problem. He on the other hand, had a damn bike that he came over on one night and decided to keep it at my house.

On one occasion I recall having some appointments to attend to and by the time I got home, he had taken all of our clothes to the Laundromat, washed and folded everything. (He was a very clean person). Though he did this, it angered me because my mom raised us saying, "don't allow a man to wash your underwear." That was a problem for me and I voiced it but he really didn't pay it any attention. He would go to the store and get whatever I needed. (I didn't realize he was keeping me in the house on purpose) When my daughter's father would come to get her, he'd always go to the door and say he'd take care of it and that her father didn't need to see me just to pick up his daughter. I would look at him as if he were crazy and think "who the hell do you think you are" but again, I blew it off and didn't pay him any attention. **WARNING SIGN**

These were all the warning signs I was overlooking being naive and silly. As time went on into the short relationship, he told me he loved me and wanted me to himself, but I didn't pay it a lot of attention (although it felt good to hear those words from a man with his character – when I say character, I mean, he was a very attractive young man, well groomed, he faithfully kept himself shaved, haircut, dressed very nice and he was a hard worker. Not that I dealt with garbage type men, but the attention that he was giving me, the way that he carried himself was different. I can't take anything away from him (he did construction work, when he was tired of hustling). He had a heart; he just didn't know he had one. Every woman throughout West Tampa, College Hill, Ponce De Leon, Jackson Height, Belmont Heights, and Central Park wanted him, but the thing that triggered him most was that, in those same areas, men wanted me. It he felt like he had to deal with competition.

He got to a point where he was infatuated with me. Sometimes we would be in the house (I've always been lots of fun in the bedroom) and I'd be doing all kind of crazy things to him and I noticed every now and then (more times than needed), he would grab the back of my hair, pull me up to his face and say "that shit right there is going to cause me to take your mother fucking head clean off." I'm crazy as hell because I was thinking he must feel that way because he's being well pleased, it was just his way of pillow talk that he was dishing out at the time. Looking back, what the hell kind of pillow talk was that. **WARNING SIGN** (*ladies be careful thinking everything in the bedroom is funny or controlling, don't mess around and let your body be a living sacrifice and cost you your life*). **Romans 12:1 warns us (I beseech you therefore, brethren, by the mercies of God, that ye present your bodies a living sacrifice, holy, acceptable unto God, which is your reasonable service ... I wasn't thinking about that** *at the time because I was in sin, having fun SO I THOUGHT!*. I began to notice where he said that entirely too much. At times he would stop in the middle of sex and grab my neck and tell me he would kill me if he found I was with someone. Here I go with my silly ass, again thinking at first, *"This dude must be really strung the hell out on this wild shit I'm doing, and I guess I may need to roll back."* He was saying it more and more during any kind of sex. I didn't like that too much anymore because he'd even say to me "Think it's a game and play with me. I'll hurt you and any *ni**a* about you." That wasn't cool with me, and I began to feel scared and controlled. When I started to pull back, that caused a bigger problem because to him that meant I must be messing with someone else since I don't do what I used to do with him and he knew my sex drive was always high. This was becoming bizarre because I was my own person doing my own thing before this man came around.

My mom didn't like him when she first met him. She said it was something about him that she didn't like but I figured it was all because he wanted me, he told me that he would protect me, he wouldn't let anyone hurt me, that he'd kill about me because he'd fallen in love with me. This is a man who said he loved me, and would kill or die for me, and I really liked that because if he would kill or die for me, that meant he really wanted to be with me, not knowing that he really meant those words literally. I was determined that I was going to keep this man and I was going to keep him happy no matter what it took. I wanted him to just love me and never leave me. Yes, in spite of the fear that I had begun to feel, in spite of the control that I was feeling, in spite of the warning signs, I just wanted to be loved. Yet, I didn't know he had a history of abuse himself and towards other people as well, and at that time in my life, I don't really know if it would have mattered if I did know because he loved me.

Chapter 5 – The First Hit!

A month or so into the relationship around March of 1991, he hit me. **"SILENT SCREAM"** I was in College Hill and had been talking to this guy named Bobby. He and Bobby didn't really like each other at all. Bobby told me that if I had any problems out of him, let him know because he would kick his ass. I asked Bobby why didn't he like him and he said because he ran his mouth too much and he talked like a girl. I laughed because I know that couldn't be the same dude, so Bobby had to be tripping and may have been jealous of him for some reason. Well he saw me talking to Bobby because when I got back to my cousins house in College Hill, and we got into the car to head home, he asked what Bobby and I were talking about. I didn't think twice about it and started telling him that Bobby said if I ever needed him, he was there. I continued to explain that I wasn't thinking about Bobby like that and then I laughed it off. I remember distinctly that we were riding down Columbus Drive, and as I was laughing, I'll never forget, he hit me with so much force; he knocked my head against the window in the car and knocked me out, I mean completely out. That was the first time he hit me, and it should not have been a red flag **WARNING SIGN**, it should have been a red flag, a red blanket, a red anything, but it definitely should have been the time to get out and away from this man right then.

My head hit the window so hard that it felt like he had shaken something loose in my head. I immediately went into a state of fear of him, and all of that talk he'd been doing had finally played itself out. That was the moment I felt lost as if a spell had instantly been placed on me. I didn't being come to my senses until we pulled into the yard, and this was only because he was pulling me out of the car. I remember sliding down to the ground with my face and head in so much pain, and him picking me up. While doing so, someone passed by and asking if he needed help with getting me into the house; I guess the person thought I was drunk, but he declined the offer and told him that he was good. I recall standing to my feet as best as I could, just enough to make it into the front door. He grabbed me, told me he was sorry, and explained that he did it because he had fallen in love with me. He continued to say that he didn't want anyone else to have me and he would kill anyone that tried to take me from him. I was in the half-conscious zone, but still was able to hear him say the words, I love you. Those words immediately hit me in my heart. The fact that someone said they loved me and loved me to a point that he would hurt someone about me, felt satisfying. Although a part of it felt good, a part of me was confused. He begins to cry, hold and comfort me until I felt better (although it appeared that he was the one that was hit more so than me, I was comforting him).

He didn't leave any scars, so it was just my memory of what

had happened, and the pain from it. Through his holding me, and his comforting, we slowly made our way to the point of having sex. This time it was different though, not in how I performed, but it was why I did it. This time it was more so out of fear. Afterwards we went to sleep and started a new day. I didn't tell anyone because they would have told me to leave him or would have thought negatively about him. They would have said malicious things, and I didn't want anyone to think badly about him *IT WAS JUST THAT ONE TIME AND HE APOLOGIZED.* I didn't want anyone to know that it was happening to me because then it would just show true that no one would ever love me because I knew better, that love was not abusive. I didn't want my mom to be right, I wasn't going to let myself be black and ugly, with no one ever wanting me. I didn't want to be a failure again, and not maintain a relationship or a man. As time went on, he still did and said little things like continue to question me about things that may have seemed trivial to me, but they were important to him. One day he slapped me in the mouth which burst the inside of my lip. He would always grab me and **HE'D APOLOGIZE**, and admit he didn't know what came over him, but he hated the thought of someone else having me. I assured him numerous times that I wouldn't step out on him, that I was content with him, but that was never enough. **WARNING SIGNS**

If I went to my parent's house, he'd show up there out of nowhere, and he would follow me to my friend's house just to sit there with us. If we talked about anything concerning men in any way, he'd look at me with a nasty look, and when we would get back home, everything that I talked about with my friends would be brought up and started a fight or argument. He started to hit me more, but when he'd hit me it would be in my arms or legs, places that wouldn't leave a mark for others to see but I knew eventually it was going to be my face. Yet, I always gave into the words "I love you." Those words seemed to comfort any rage that was inside of me because I wanted to be loved for real. I wanted to feel what love was like, and I enjoyed the soft kisses. He made sure to be very attentive to my body, and he took his time with everything that he did, with me and to me, while he was slowly killing me and I didn't see it. Whenever he'd hit me and I would say that we should not be together, he would say to me that he was the only one that has ever loved me. He always reminded me that my mom had never loved me and would never love me, and the fact that my mom said I would never get a man to love me because I was ugly. In spite of all that, he would say that he loved me regardless of what anyone said about me because I was pretty, and very special to him. Well of course I would fall right back into his arms because he was feeding a huge void. It's the same one that I use to fill with dancing, drinking and so-called drugging. Now I had a man to show to my mom that at least I had a man and he loved me even if he beat me. I figured that it had to be the reason why she hated him so much because like he professed to me, he really loved me and that was something that she hated. The abuse went on for months to come. I was kicked, spit on, hit with the back of the gun, and I had to do things sexually that I didn't want to do, with him there were no limits. It was sick for so many reasons, I didn't dare say anything because I didn't want him to leave me and find it in someone else, but most of all because I didn't want to be beat for saying no. Some days, if he was feeling really jumpy, he would beat me so bad that I would not be able to see out of either of my eyes, move my mouth, or just sit up straight. **"SILENT SCREAMS"** I endured a lot of pain during these months, and as much as my mental and emotional state was use to feeling pain. (Remember from the first book.), I had two kids, but yet I was a child to him myself. I felt I couldn't scold my kids in a motherly manner because I had a man scolding me, but thanks be to God, my children still respected me.

Chapter 6 – Too Afraid to Even Trust God

I had lost myself in this man. He was my god, my drug, my parents, he was literally my life. I couldn't go to bed, I couldn't take a bath, brush my teeth, take birth control pills, have a telephone, open my blinds in the house, go outside my house, have friends, talk to people when we were out, laugh at jokes, without his permission. If we were out with other people standing around laughing and talking, I couldn't laugh with them unless he gave me a signal of approval. If someone asked me a question, I wasn't able to answer until he said it was okay with him. It wasn't public; it was a certain glance he would give me to know if I could talk or if it would be better if I kept my mouth shut. *You have to understand, I that was tired of fighting with him and I did not want to take anymore abuse if I did not have to.* The most serious part to that is the fact that I was actually afraid of him now.

At times, when we would walk places together, and I had to either keep my eyes on him or look straight ahead. I was not allowed turn my head to the left or the right *(that's funny, sounds like the scripture in the bible Deuteronomy 5:32 Ye shall observe to do therefore as the Lord your God hath commanded you: ye shall not turn aside to the right hand or the left)* or as a consequence, he would hit me, and that was out in the in the streets. I was so fearful of this man. I don't know if Love was what I was feeling anymore because I had so much fear inside of me. **"SILENT SCREAMS."** Before I met him I was modeling lingerie, selling dope, partying, hanging out and just enjoying life. I was weighing 155 pounds and in less than three months of being in a relationship with him I was down to 113 pounds. The doctors thought I had AIDS because of the drastic drop of weight, and on top of the weight loss, I got pregnant. I didn't care about any of these issues because at times I wanted to die on account the beatings. I never knew stress could take you to that point, but I learned rather quickly. I was so stressed out that I began to break out with little bumps all over my body. I would itch like crazy, only to find out that it was stress that had given me a bad rash to my skin because it wasn't nourished or healthy anymore.

Chapter 7 - God What Have I Gotten Myself Into?

Some nights I would walk the streets all night long with my child, especially the nights he would use the car and not come back home until late. Remember I had two kids; my oldest son had been living with my parents since birth, so he wasn't around to witness the physical abuse that often. On the nights when I wouldn't walk the streets all night and my car wasn't working, I would sleep in the city parks like, Ray Park, MacFarlane, or anywhere else that I could, just so that he wouldn't beat on me. **"SILENT SCREAMS"** I was beyond tired of being beat almost every night. One night he jumped on me and I ran and left the house. My daughter was at her grandmother's house, so I didn't have to worry about her, so I towards Main Street where I ran into Gangster and some of the other guys that knew me and heard what I was going through. They sensed something was wrong, and they wanted to go back to the house and beat him half to death, but I didn't want them to get into any trouble for the choices I'd made. I was just that person that didn't put others in my business. I didn't want anyone getting hurt because of my choices in life so I asked them to please just take me somewhere. Gangster and Marlon took me to get a hotel room for the night just to get away from the madness.

There was another situation where for one week he beat me every night for no reason. I was too afraid to call the police because he would constantly tell me that he would get out and how he would kill me when he did. Nevertheless, I carried through and continued to pray. I still didn't really know who God was, but I knew that I had to pray and I knew someone was praying for me. Even while I was pregnant the abuse didn't stop. He would never harm the kids physically, and always showed them love and protection, except for the fact that he was beating their mom and inflicting mental and emotional abuse on their little minds, he was alright. During this time, so much of my prayer life was starting to resurface. The person that used to be wild and crazy had slowly died. All the prayers, and church, that I had so greatly needed was becoming a reality to me. Now it was urgent that I use that prayer that had been instilled in me by my grandmother and spiritual mother. I also needed my Mother Gooden; no one could anoint and pray for me like my mommy. All the times that I was around that high yellow woman and her family she was praying and anointing my head. She would tell me that God is going to use me, and I needed to hear that from her. I needed that woman that used to roll her eyes up in her head and speak life into my spirit. I needed her to call those things that were not as though they were, but I didn't know where or how to find her **OH BUT GOD!**

As time went on, I slowly began to meet more of his family; each time there would be someone that would always whisper and tell me that I wasn't the type of woman for him, and that I'd better get out of this relationship with him before it was too late. I didn't understand why they told me that AT FIRST. He would repeatedly tell me how his family always outcast him, then he began to explain to me bits and pieces of his childhood. Yet no matter how many times I saw his little sister or his mom, they would unhesitatingly beg me to get out of the relationship with him. I found myself getting mad with them because I felt they were cruel for feeling that way about their own flesh and blood. At that time I didn't know what they meant, however, later on in the relationship I understood just why they felt the way they did because this man didn't care who he fought me in front of.

One specific time we were walking down Main St. and a guy complimented me (all he said was I was very pretty, ok, maybe that was something the guy shouldn't have said but maybe he should've dealt with the dude, not me). He slapped me and was ready to fight the guy; he told the guy that he should have given him the compliment not me. I was just outdone on that one. He tried to fight me in front of his mom one day at her house, and she grabbed the broom and tried to beat him senseless. She then called the police and asked them to take me and my daughter home. He just didn't care or have any regard anymore. He would follow me everywhere I went, even when I went to my First Lady (Momma Davy) home for prayer. When he followed me there she really had to pray because she wanted to do him in, he followed me because he thought I would leave him or find someone else (after you buddy, I'll take single for 500 ALEX) ☺

Chapter 8 - Praying For My Kids and My Life

This is a man that didn't even care how he beat me in front of the kids. My oldest daughter saw more than any of the other kids (due to her age). This is a man that would kick me down to the ground with his steel toe boots on (out of nowhere). I found myself having to fold on the ground to prevent him from kicking me in the face, so I'd curl into a fetal position to save my face. My oldest daughter would stand there screaming begging and pleading with him to leave me alone, but he would only stop long enough to put her in the room and shut the door. She could still hear (what I tried to muffle within **"SILENT SCREAMS"** the cries and shouts of him yelling and saying that I'm cheating on him or where is the man hiding, calling me whores, and every degrading name one could think of. I remember sometimes, I would get my Bible, and all the teachings out of the word that had been spoken into my spirit from childhood started to rise up. The memories of my mom sending us to church every Sunday, my Grandma Bells' home church, and going to church with my maternal and paternal family, Grandma Sue, Mother Gooden, and Ms. Sheridan all came running back to my mind. I knew prayer was instilled in me in spite of the life I had encountered. I just didn't know God was the man with the plans for my life, but

I continued to pray every night that God would not let him come in and beat me, but before I could get off of my knees he would come in the door from his drugs, women and streets and for no reason, punch me in the face. That was the place he wanted to hurt me most. Every night as it became routine, I had to get on my knees and take his shoes off. If I wasn't going fast enough he would get one foot and put in on my thigh and the other foot and kick me backwards. **"SILENT SCREAMS"** The only thing I could do was get up and continue to take them off because I knew what was next. Most times after I got his shoes off, I had to undress him and while he stand there, I'd be on my knees and have to perform oral sex on him until he told me to stop. Next, I had to follow him through the house while he inspected all the rooms to make sure that no one was in the house. If I took one wrong move he would turn and punch me. There are numerous times he would turn and kick me until I collapsed, then he would result to kicking me in my back, face or anywhere that I didn't cover up. He hallucinated a lot when he was on the drugs, and to witness a person hallucinate was one of the wildest experiences I ever encountered.   He would sometimes come in, get the scissors and cut my clothes off of me because he would say I had been with other men and I was nasty. I was too afraid to cry, run, fight or scream. **"SILENT SCREAM"** You know how parents are with their children sometimes, we tell them things like, *you better hush* *that fuss* or *you better not come in here with that crying.* Well I was like that with him; I was like the child awaiting instructions from a parent. He'd sleep with the gun right by my head in his hands and I would be so afraid to move. He slept with his legs and arms around me so that I couldn't move out of the bed.

He hallucinated so bad when he was on drugs, that every so often he would come in the house and start looking in the refrigerator, the cabinets, under the bed and everywhere saying that there was a man in the house. He would get a chair out of the kitchen, sit in the hall way in between the middle of the bedroom doors with the gun in his hands having me and the kids lay in the same bed afraid to move. Every now and then he would jump up and run towards what he thought was a shadow, which wasn't really there, all due to his hallucination. He would come in the room, get me out of bed, and would even make me squat there in front of him and not move so he could watch my mouth to see if it moved. Then he would punch me in my mouth because he said he saw my mouth move and I was giving the 'invisible' man oral sex right there in front of him. He has literally attacked me trying to get this so-called man off of me. There have been situations when I would be in the kitchen cooking and he would come in and say he saw a man. Out of the blue he would strike me across my shoulder blade with the butt of the gun and knock me to my knees. Then he would force me over the kitchen sink, and have sex making sure with every forceful stroke there was pain. "SILENT SCREAMS" meanwhile I had to act as if I enjoyed every moment of it as tears slowly rolled down my face. He was someone who was literally **Loving Me to Death**. I was angry with God because I felt my prayers were in vain, but the Lord was grieving with me the entire time. I had more faith in that worldly god than I had in the Spiritual God, so I had God's hands tied. *{Scripture reads: James 2:26, For as the body without the spirit is dead, so faith without works is dead also.}* God was keeping me alive and I didn't realize it then, but a lot of people die in this mess. I will never forget the night I heard a voice say to me as I was praying *"This is for my glory just hold on to my unchanging hands."* I remember saying out loud in anger, *"How are you going to get glory out of me being beaten like a dog."* The voice said back to me, *"I know you are angry and I know you don't understand right now, but I am with you and I won't let you die. Be strong in the Lord and I will bring you out. I am going to use your situation to raise you up before people and for my glory and to take you into great places for my name sake."* I thought it was the devil because I wanted to know how I was going to be used by being beaten day in and day out. Yet, a little while longer and he ended up going to jail for an unrelated crime that had nothing to do with me , but still domestic violence) I married him in jail, and **you ask why I married him in jail when**

I had a way out. I was under the impression that he was getting out because the person wasn't pressing charges. I was pregnant, but most of all, I didn't know if I could function out on my own anymore, since he had controlled my life for so long which caused me to be lost in his world. I was still fearful and knowing one day he'd be out and I was stuck with him for life, I felt there was no way out. **"SILENT SCREAM"** I sent him to jail a few times, but back then you could go down and drop the charges. I did so because I was afraid he would get out and kill me and I was also, dependent on him. I didn't know how to operate out in the real world without him. (Still not knowing if Love is what I was feeling.) I thought I would die without him there to control everything I did. Paying bills, leaving the house, when to get up, when to go to bed, when to cook and when to bathe were some of the many so-called struggles I was facing that were once so basic to me, I had lost control of how to help myself…I was in his prison! At the end of court he ended up getting a three year prison sentence, and I was lost because now I didn't know how I was going to maintain myself without his control. Without that worldly god, I knew I had to lean on someone and I was too afraid to get another man.

When my lease in my duplex was up I moved further away from everyone because I was ashamed of my life and I was pregnant abused and wasn't the fighter that I used to be. I was a nobody! Not long after I moved I had my first child from him and was even more lost. My baby was born with what the doctors told me, a little drugs in her system...I never thought that the fathers drug use could affect the baby. The doctor said that, because of his heavy drug use, it was his seed that was in me, so of course the seed would have the drugs. She wasn't bad off though. She just couldn't hear loud noises and she would cry all night long. This cause me to walk on egg shells around the house. By this time, my mom started to come around me and she'd even drive all the way out to my house. I actually think she felt sorry for me, so I figured she did love me a little bit somewhere deep inside of everything else that she normally showed. My mom would come over and sit at my house for a while and when my baby had hemorrhoid problems or any sickness she came to check her and help me out. I felt so good just to have her there.

Chapter 9 - When the Cat is Away, the Mouse Will Play

Time did go on and I slowly started to get my strength and I met this guy while I was in the store. This guy tried to talk to me, but I was afraid to talk to him (it felt like my husband was able to watch me from the prison walls). I didn't realize this guy lived in the same complex that I lived in, but he kept telling me I was pretty and so were my girls. I modestly smiled and held my head down. (Because my tooth was partially out of my mouth) He went on to ask me why I held my head down, I plainly responded, "no reason." He continued to ask where my man was and I told him that my husband was in prison. He proceeded to tell me how I needed a man to take care of me while he was away but I was persistent in walking and trying to ignore him. Still, this man followed me through the store (I'd pushed my kids to the store in the stroller). I told the guy that I just didn't want to be bothered and that I wasn't the type of woman he wanted to talk to. {You have to know, this man had started calling me fat, ugly, black, no good, trifling, telling me no man is ever going to want me but him, no man will ever love me but him and if a man got with me, it would only be for sex}.

Everything that my husband use to say just resurfaced my childhood, so I protected myself by telling men that I wasn't the kind of girl that they wanted because I felt like I was worthless. I literally told men that about myself; but this guy wouldn't take that for an answer. He said to me, "I'm not sure what man has hurt and lied to you baby girl, but you are beautiful. Don't let any man bring you that far down". I still didn't give in, but I did smile and he said, "Well I did get a little smile out of you." He went to the cashier, paid for his stuff and wrote his number on a piece of paper. He said, "Call me if you ever need a friend" and told my daughters, "bye little ladies, take care of your beautiful mommy". I felt so good but still at the same time ugly and afraid. I took the number and looked at it, but I wouldn't use it. I immediately called my friend Brina and told her about it. She came down to see me, she lived up the street and as you can see, Brina was always there for me. Brina told me I needed to at least talk as a friend just to relieve my mind. I ran into this guy again, and he complimented me just as before. So I finally talked to him and invited him over to my house. We started talking for a while and it was nice. He began to build my self-esteem up and I was at last starting to feel good about myself. My mom and family met this guy and they really liked him. He called my mom "momma" and it was nice, it felt like this guy really liked me. Welp to my surprise we couldn't go any further due to the fact that he was married, by the way, so was I. Financially he made sure I had what I wanted and that felt pleasing but also so new to me. Within a few months, he'd given me the money to get my mouth fixed, so I went and got gold put in my mouth to finally hide that ugly broken tooth that he knocked out.

Time went on and I started just hanging out again, I started feeling positive about myself and my self-esteem had pulled up a little, yes I still had my bad days, especially when I had to pull the tooth out when I brushed my teeth. Through it all, I always had that support of my sister Brina. She was always on my side throughout the madness and if anyone endured this with me, it was her (thanks Brina). While feeling myself, I started dating this other guy that I used to talk to before I met my husband, who was also the same one I was in the College Hill seeing the first night I took my husband home. The guy that built me up was slowly starting to grow out of my system so I wasn't seeing him as much. I just couldn't keep doing the married man thing knowing how it must have affected her as well, remembering I'm married as well. She and I finally got into a word splash and that wasn't my cup of tea, so slowly I pulled away from him. I would still see him every now and then until it completely died away.

When my lease was up, I moved to Sulphur Springs, and was still dating the old but new guy, my kids were getting older and it wasn't so bad. Yet for some reason my oldest daughter really had hatred towards the new baby; I'm not sure if it was because it was my abusive husband child or, if she was jealous because it was normally the both of us unless my oldest son came over. I'm not sure what the problem was because she would try to hurt the baby by doing things liking pulling her off the sofa and the bed, she did anything she could to hurt her.

Slowly I was getting tired of the crazy life and I knew that the time was winding down for my husband to come home from prison and for me to go back in his prison, because again, I felt because he was my husband, I had to stay with him. I started to go into a mental slump again because he was coming out to begin a work release program. I was so nervous and it was still a few months before that time came but it was too close for my mental state. I would toss and turn wondering if I was going to be strong this time around.

When he got to work release, I used to go visit him I was still constantly nervous because I was still so afraid of him. Those fears just immediately weld up in me again. Right before he got out I moved to Highland Pines near my cousin Al (which gave me some security because I wasn't so far alone). My cousin and I had a lot of fun hanging at each other's house. I was talking to a guy that lived over there but it was nothing serious. My little cousin/god-daughter Toya was to my house quite a bit before my husband got back home. My family and I always just hung at my house sitting under the carport barbecuing and just having a good time. Although in our minds we knew that all of this wouldn't last long because he would be getting out and my life would change again. I felt like I was obligated to take him back because he was my husband and by right that's what I needed to do, even though he was abusive.

Of course the work release time was done and over too soon, and it was time for him to come home. It didn't take long before the control started again. It started because he had heard that I was messing around on him while he was in prison. We went back and forth with that for a while and he used that as his excuse to come home cheating again. The abuse didn't start right away at the house I was staying in but I knew it wouldn't be long so I still continued to pray (still unsure how to trust God). He was clean and just maybe he had changed (in my heart I knew that wasn't true). I got pregnant again after about a month of him being out (with our second child together).

Not long after that the hitting started up again, despite the fact that I was pregnant, this man still continued to beat me. I called the police and he went to jail but I already knew he would only stay for like 2 months or 3 at the most. I was sad because Toya was still always around my oldest daughter and it's unfortunate that both of them had to witness so many days and nights of running and fighting and I didn't want anyone to know or see that part of my life, Toya looked up to me. I felt like I was dying again, I felt like I was going back into that same rut and didn't know which way to turn. He was in jail again, I was pregnant and I was so in need of my spiritual mother until it was unreal. She was the only woman that really knew how to pray for me.

Chapter 10 - I Need My Spiritual Mother!

I started needing my spiritual mother again like never before but I didn't even know where to begin to look for her, but I began to pray, I needed to see her, I need to feel her touch on my face. After a few months went by I ran into her at a Walgreens and I almost lost my mind when I saw her, I ran and jumped towards her lying in her arms, I was outdone with joy. She told me how to get in touch with her, can you believe she lived right around the corner from me all this time and I couldn't wait to call her and be with her. Once I called her I got under her wings again, he was still in jail and I had my mommy back. I started going to church with her, and I gave my life to the true and living God. Even then it was for the wrong reasons because I needed something or someone to pacify that void that was left by him. Never realizing that God had already started filling that void, I just knew it felt good to have that feeling that was being manifested within me. The feeling of real worship, the attention that I was getting from the congregation and how they loved on me, it felt great. After going to the church with my spiritual mommy for a while, I received the baptism of the Holy Ghost while I was pregnant and got baptized in the name of Jesus!

I felt like a new woman while going to church, but I still didn't truly and fully know God yet or His true powers and desire for me. Now I was slowly starting to feel good, I was breathing a different kind of air. I was praying for my husband, praying for my family, praying over my unborn child and had a connection with God because I had the Holy Ghost with the evidence of speaking in tongues.

Well that time came and my husband got out of jail, he came home and I introduced him to my spiritual mom and she immediately picked up things were not right in her spirit. She would say certain things to me, which caused me to open up to her about the abuse. She started really praying about the situation and even praying for him. He became pretty close to my spiritual mother (although he didn't know at that time she was the relative to the people that I was raised in the streets with). He confided in her with things, but even still trying to make it seem like things where my fault. She was very blunt about what she needed to say, and she didn't allow him to try and blame me for the abuse. I was in church quite a bit trying to change my life for the better and raise my kids for the better. My husband got into more trouble on an unrelated crime towards someone else and ended up going to jail before I had our second child.

Thankfully, my church family was behind me 100% and it felt precious to bring my baby into the world in the church. I was singing in the choir, doing praise and worship, working the altar and just all over the church participating in activities and it felt good. I was in church so much until that was my safe place.

As always, he got out and I took him back, and the abuse started all over again. When he went to church with me, there was always a problem if I sat in the front row, I was trying to get someone's attention, if I sat in the middle row I was trying to show someone who he was, if I sat in the back row I was hiding and ashamed of him and it all end in a fight. He always watched as most of the men in the church supported me and felt I was a strong woman of God. He had questions about most of the Deacons that he accused me of; he even accused me of my Pastor at Victory. He also had a big problem with Dea. Tony, because he didn't like the way Tony looked at me. Dea. Tony also lived with my Spiritual Mom and that was really a problem for him. That didn't make me leave church, I was determined to hold on to my walk with the Lord even if I went to church wrinkled after sleeping in the car all night Sis. Ferguson would always fix me up. I enjoyed church in spite of all that I was going through, it was the only place I felt peace even in the midst of the storm. Some weekend, in order to make it to church the kids and I would sleep in the car and make the best of it.

REFLECTIONS
Chapter 11 - The Sexual Abuse

My husband had a sex disorder; he felt that he needed sex twenty-four hours a day. When we first got together that didn't bother me because I was enduring the same sex demon. People better know there is such a demonic sex demon. Seems as if I could never be satisfied by one man or any man for that matter. I could sleep with multiple men in one day, go home and masturbate and still not be satisfied, my sex drive was crazy (although someone reading this might be excited about it, honey it's a spirits that's out of control TRUST ME) so his sexual addiction didn't disturb me to any extent. It was just he had no limits to his sex. Although, I had the same sex demon that he had, and was willing to try anything that came my way, it was the fact of being forced to do things that was an entirely different ball game. He and I connected well within our sexual relationship because for once both of us found satisfaction within each other.

The time when I first endured anal sex, **"SILENT SCREAM"**, it was a wild and painful experience; I was so afraid of him that night. He was on drugs that night, and mixed the fact that we had conversations in the past about anal sex, I think that had him all confused mentally. I had told him that I had never tried it and had no intentions on trying it, but to be honest, I did tell him that one day I might try it, but I laughed it off. He let me know that was something he enjoyed doing and he wanted me to try it with him. I brushed it off because he wasn't high when we first talked about it, so I dismissed it and merely said "Yeah one day." He still mentioned it a few more times, but I over talked it each time.

He came in high that particular night (the first time he did it to me) and as usual I had to walk around the house with him while he looked through to make sure no one was there. Then, I had to go in the room with him while he sat on the dresser and continued to use the rest of the cocaine that he didn't use before he made it home. I had to sit there and watch him use it, (while praying within) I begged him to just throw the rest away. At that moment he called me over to him and when I went to him he punched and knocked me back onto the bed. **"SILENT SCREAM"**, I got up and went back to him another time and he did it again (you have to understand, I was TERRIFIED of this man), I had to go back over to him, after he finally finished snorting his cocaine, and the time had finally come, he wanted anal sex. I tried to talk him out of it, but as usual he was high, and I had no win, for whatever reason, when someone is on drugs, they have an unusual strength. (I knew that it wouldn't be something that he would take his time doing because he was high) I sat on the side of the bed with hidden tears running down my face. **"SILENT SCREAM"** He always put my daughter in the other room when he was acting up, even though she could still hear everything that was going on.

I was so nervous because I didn't know what was next. He took my clothes off of me and naturally I had to do the normal pleasing of oral sex. It was having oral sex with him until he got hard. I was still crying as I continued with oral sex on him. **"SILENT SCREAM"** Finally, he made me stop and get on my knees facing the bed. (I thought I was going to shake into little pieces because I was so sacred, tears streaming down my face, wanting to die, wanting to be numb all over). He was behind me on his knees while in my ear telling me to bend over and that he wasn't going to hurt me. He tried to assure me that the anal sex wasn't going to hurt because it's not that bad, and I would just have to get used to it. He put Vaseline all over his penis and began to try to penetrate me and I kept telling him that it was hurting. I couldn't go on because it was too painful, but he carried on and told me to just brace myself. He said it was already going in and I just needed to relax. (But that was so hard for me to do and so far from the truth) I began to scream to the top of my lungs begging him to please stop because I couldn't bear the pain.

"SILENT SCREAM"

The more I screamed and cried, the more he kept forcing himself into me. He pushed my face in the pillow so I wouldn't wake up my daughter. I begged him to stop but the more I pleaded the more he forced himself inside of me with his arm pushing into my back so that I wouldn't move, the more I try to shut my body down, the harder and more forceful he became. **"SILENT SCREAM"** Finally when he got his orgasm he kissed me on the neck, told me he loved me, got up and said, "See, it wasn't that bad, now go to the bathroom and clean yourself up." I wanted to die, I was speechless and in disbelief with what just happened. I felt like I had just been raped (and I was), I felt dirty and embarrassed, my stomach wrenched with so much pain. After a short period of time, I got strength to get off of my knees, make it to the bathroom and clean myself up. I looked in on my daughter and went back into the room with him so he could put his leg and arm around me with the gun, to know when I got out of the bed. **"SILENT SCREAM"**

Chapter 12 - Make It Go Away!

One night he got home, and was so high he couldn't get the key into the door. He must have gotten frustrated because he began kicking the door and yelling for me to open it. I jumped up and ran to the door because I could hear the anger in his voice, I knew without a doubt he was going to beat me this night; I got the door open and he immediately closed fist me across the glass table in the living room. I made an attempt to crawl backwards away from him **"SILENT SCREAM"**, but he came in on me so fast I couldn't get away, I recall, him kicking and hitting me as I do my normal fetal position fold. He said I changed the locks on the door so that my boyfriend could come over to be with me. **"SILENT SCREAM"** I never had the opportunity to say anything because I would really get beat then. He began to search the house and as usual I had to follow him. When he turned around and notice I was walking too far behind him, he hit me, calling me fat, ugly dumb and stupid. He got the scissors and cut my clothes off of me in the middle of the hallway, hit me and knocked me back to the floor. As he kicked me again I fold so he wouldn't hit my face. (The place he wanted to hurt me the most) I was always scared when he got the scissors to cut my clothes off because I never knew if or when he was going to eventually stab me as he threatened to do so many times, (praise God he never did).

I recall one night I was hiding at a friend Andrea's house and her boyfriend told him I was there. When he got there, he was so high, he came into the room with a full quart of beer in his hands; he sat on the chair in front of the bed, I set up while holding my daughter (she was asleep on top of me so I thought) he told me he felt like splitting my face to the white meat with the beer bottle and I started to cry and beg him quietly not to hit me with the bottle because I had my child in my lap. On top of that, he would have killed me with the first blow from the impact of a full quart bottle of beer.   I don't really know if I cared about dying, I just didn't want to die in my 3 year old daughters arms with blood all over her. When I realized the gun was under the bed, I pulled the gun and told him if he didn't move I'd kill him. He knew that I wasn't going to do anything for the sake of my daughter. I tried to roll my daughter off of me but she started to cry and held on to my shirt. I stood from the bed, and we started to fight over the gun, Andrea and her boyfriend came running in and got the gun and put him out the house, I ran back to my baby as she just lay there crying.

There were numerous nights when my daughter and I slept outside in my next door neighbors shed until she got home from the club. My baby saw so many roaches and rats back there where the washer and dryer were, it was the shed. When my neighbor would get home, I'd see her light and tap her back window and she would let us go through her window and into her house. We had to get out of there because one night I didn't answer the door and he kicked the hinges off the back door and knocked the entire door down. Some nights when I would hear him pull up in the drive way; my daughter and I would jump out the window and go next door to my friend Patrice's house. We would just lie in her house and listen to him knock on her door looking for us knocking harder as we lay in her room really quiet until he left.

I'd always try to go to her house when I knew he was coming home high, when he wasn't home a certain hour, I already knew what to expect and I'd go to her early so I would have somewhere to go and it would prevent me from getting beat that night, I was tired. When we got home the next day, and down off of his high, I would tell him why I left. He would do the normal routine which was to cry, say he was sorry **HE APOLOGIZED**. Yet he still said he didn't have a drug and alcohol problem. He wasn't always a bad person but 75% to 85% of the time he was, and I'm sure you're saying YEAH RIGHT geesh 75 to 85% bad lady really!

On occasions I would to have to give him oral sex until he

came down off of his high, rather that meant ten minutes, thirty minutes or longer, at least it felt as though it lasted that long. Sometimes I'd suck on him for so long that the inside of my jaw began to tear, my lips swelled, and my mouth was sore, but if I stopped he would hit me. Sex or oral sex was the only thing that would make him began to calm down or put him to sleep. His is sex drive was extremely high so he would have sex nonstop for hours until he got sleepy. **"SILENT SCREAM"**

He jumped on me one night because my mouth was so sore and I couldn't suck anymore, so he hit me in my mouth and broke my front tooth. Afterwards, he cried more than I did, saying he was sorry **HE APOLOGIZED**. He was always sorry, and always crying! I can recall the first time he forced me to let him perform oral sex on me YES FORCED ME TO ALLOW HIM. Getting oral sex from him was something I never wanted for the simple fact that he beat me all the time when he hallucinated for thinking I was with other men or had given other men his body as he called and referred to my body his body. I knew if he were to give me oral sex, it would still be trouble, he would feel like he was putting his mouth on me and I was sleeping with other men, then he'd jumps on me.

He was high that particular night, and this time he wanted to do it to me, I begged him not to, and that almost got me beat. He thought I was saying no because I had been with someone, so he forced me to let him do it to prove to him I hadn't been with anyone else. I was not allowed to use the bathroom after sex, because he said I was trying to urinate out any babies that I might be getting pregnant with. Many times I tried to explain to him that once you are pregnant, you're pregnant, and you can't pee the babies out, nonetheless, he didn't like for me to use the bathroom after sex. Not only could I not shower, brush my teeth and so many other things before he got home, he had to smell my underwear as soon as I took them off, when it was that time of the month and I didn't want to have sex, he had to stand in the bathroom and watch me change in order to see proof due to the fact he wanted to make sure I wasn't lying. (Although sometimes he still forced me to have sex during that time of the month anyway). On top of all this abuse, he cheated with so many women.

Chapter 13 - He's Going to Kill Me

I'll never forget the time when I had just given birth to my little girl from him; he got out of jail during my 6 weeks after birth. I had been hiding from him for a few days and found out he was looking for me. When he finally found me he was so high, and began to hit me. My baby was only a few days old, and he was demanding that I have sex with him. I kept refusing because I had just had the baby. I wasn't well and I still had lots of bleeding, and he beat me so bad that day. I tried to run away, but only made it as far as the front door. He dragged me from the front yard to the backyard, and hit me in the face with his fist so hard, it knocked me completely out. I remember him waking me up by spraying water in my face with the water hose as I laid there in the mud. When he realized that I had come to, he pulled me up by my hair, dragging me into the house and turned the shower on and made me wash the mud from my hair and body. When I got out of the shower, he made me do sexual things that I didn't want to do as always. He did not have any remorse in his heart or his eyes. He raped me and I had just had my baby. My body was still healing because of the baby; however I couldn't cry, say or do anything. **"SILENT SCREAMS"** When he fell asleep I quietly got the baby up and left to call the police. I had made it to my doctors' office that was also a personal friend of mine, we called the police and sent them to the house, once the police got to the house, my husband answered the door and pretended to be my brother, and told the police that my husband was gone. When the policed called my doctor back to tell her what had taken place, she informed the police that they had just let my husband go; they went back and of course he was gone so they put a warrant out for his arrest. As the days went on he continued to harass and threaten me over the phone. He would come to bother me at the house when he felt like it, and even stay when he felt like it. I was so afraid of him that I felt it was pointless to call the police since they couldn't seem to catch him. If they didn't catch him, then he would know I called and give him motive to jump on me. He almost took my life a couple of nights after the water hose incident. My baby was maybe a couple of weeks old at this time. He said someone told him I had been with another man. Upset with what he had heard, I saw a look in his eyes that I had never seen before, it was like the look of death with a smile of anger in his face all in one. He came in and threw a gallon of water at me while I was holding the baby. He then got the phone with intentions on hitting me, but hit the baby instead. He tried to get to me, but stumbled and that's when I got up with the baby in my arms and I ran. I fell to the ground on top of the baby; it was only the Lord that lifted me up off the ground, into the gate of my neighbor's house. I was at her door screaming and right as he got to the door to reach me, she opened the door and I ran in. It was no one but God that kept me from dying that night. He was in a rage that I had not seen in him before and he told me I was going to die. By the time the police got there he was gone of course. They insisted that I go to the hospital with the baby just in case the phone fractured something when it hit her in the face.   When we got to the hospital, he called as well as had his girlfriend to call (and yes we were still married at the time) to see if the baby was hurt or not but the hospital had strict orders not to give out any information on the baby or myself, we were in a protective custody at the hospital and my other kids were at my cousins house.

Once released from the hospital, he tried to find me but I was hiding at my cousin's house with my kids for a few days, she's moved to Progress Village. I eventually went home because everyone was talking about me having to stay at other people's houses running from this demon. I went home alone first, just to make sure everything was secure for the kids and myself. To my surprise he had broken into my house when I wasn't home and was sitting on the sofa with the gun when I walked in the door. I couldn't turn around to run, I was in shock.   Thinking quickly, I smiled at him and asked what he was doing sitting in the house in the dark, that he's startled me. He called me over to him and I was nervous seeing the gun in his lap. He asked me to sit on his lap facing him, so I did. He didn't move the gun so I was actually sitting on top of the gun (saying to myself "Lord don't let this man shoot me between my legs"), he pulled me face to face with him and kissed me, told me how much he loved me but would also kill me dead.

I used the fact that he was coming down to my advantage and told him that I loved him and would never do anything to hurt or cause him to kill me. I begin to kiss him and lift his shirt off him, I teased and told him I couldn't undress him if the gun was in the way; he allowed me to move the gun and put it on the side of us. This was one time I was going to make sure I gave him all that I could in order for him to go to sleep and for me to stay safe. I made love to him; we laughed and played with each other. He wanted me to put on lingerie, he wanted more sex, I made sure to pick out one that he liked a lot and I danced for him as he requested, with more sex. I had to be careful not to upset him because I didn't want to trigger him.

Finally he drifted off to sleep with his leg and arm around me. I managed to get up and get out of the house because I was tired now and I knew it wouldn't be long before he killed me. I made a police report for him breaking into the house, but they didn't catch him right away. A lot of nights we couldn't stay home because he would break into the house. There was nothing I could do, it seemed like he was unstoppable. I never gave up on prayer, although a lot of times I wanted to. They finally caught him, and he got sentenced to six months, which he may have served three of those, and was out to do the same thing again. When my lease was up in Highland Pines, I moved near Seminole Heights, I got pregnant with my first son from him. The beatings never stopped, he would tell me that my son was not his baby.

One particular day he came in and was accusing me of being with my oldest two kid's father. I'd not spoken to the man but his mind told him I was involved with him. He started acting up and going into a rage, he pushed me down inside the playpen that was set up for the baby. I got away from him and ran out the door, he came after me but I was able to go back inside through another door and lock him out. He blocked one door and began to kick the other door in, I had to jump out of the window and run to the grocery store to call the police, all the while praying that I didn't lose my baby. When the police arrived, he was nowhere to be found. Time went on and I went in labor with our son, he went to the hospital with me and helped bring his son into the world, he cut the cord and held him first, naming him after himself. After I went to sleep, he left the hospital, went to get high and never came back. Two days later, I had to get a ride from the hospital, and he was home in the bed asleep. He had broken the window to get in because the keys to the house were at the hospital with me.

Chapter 14 – Falling Apart Slowly

Stress had me so messed up to the point where I broke out with small bumps all over my arms and face. At one time I thought it was eczema or mumps, until the doctor said it was a rash that was caused by severe stress. I had a nervous breakdown in April of 1998. My baby was 2 ½ weeks old when it happened. I remember being home with the kids for spring break. I was trying to cook for the kids, fix baby bottles, listen to my husband yell, and the baby was crying because he was hungry. I was physically and mentally exhausted. I was stressed beyond repair. (Thank God for the Holy Ghost), My husband was yelling and I had 6 kids in the house to tend to (I had my step-son as well) I don't know what happened, from that point, but through the Holy Ghost I remember most of the event that took place. I was out of my physical self, but the Spirit of God was there and wouldn't let me go. I remember screaming to the top of my lungs and started throwing things as my daughter told me.

I clutched tight to my baby and didn't want to let him go. I remember knocking down things in the kitchen, and snatching down the clothes in the closet. With one hand clutching my baby and the other hand I began to take my clothes off, running and screaming through the house. I felt like I needed to be free I just wanted to go, I wanted to disappear into the earth, I wanted to run away but I didn't know where to go, I wanted to take my skin off, run and never look back but I couldn't put my baby down. It was like I felt smothered, like the walls had closed in on me and I just wanted to be relieved. I managed to get out the door and began to run up the highway while still taking my clothes off screaming that I just wanted to be free. My kids cried while watching everything out the window. My husband finally caught up with me and wrestled me to the ground to try to cover me up. I guess I was fighting too much; he managed to get the baby out of my hands, and pull me slowly back to the house. Once I got inside, I guess he gave my baby to the kids, and I remember climbing under the glass table. I didn't want to be touched I wanted to be free of everything. My husband tried to move the glass table but I ran away to only hide myself under the rocking chair. I can remember hearing my husband tell me to get up because I was doing this to get attention and that I just wanted him to get him in trouble. I recall him yelling at the kids, telling them to go back in the room and to be quiet (because they kept crying and wanted to know what was wrong with me). He wouldn't stop yelling at me as if I was intentionally going through this ordeal. I couldn't move from under the rocking chair. I stayed there until the paramedics got there and pull me from under the chair and laid me in the bed. They started trying to ask me questions about what happened, but I was literally out of myself. I was still able to hear and feel everything that was going on. I could hear the paramedics asking if I was on any drugs or if I could possibly by on anything. I could hear my husband explaining to them what happened and they explained that I was having a nervous breakdown that I needed to be taken to the hospital right away. I was trying so hard to fight and get out of what was going on, but it was almost as if I was in control but still out of control, like an out of body experience. I was scared, I couldn't speak, I couldn't walk, and I was just out of it. Finally my dad came in the door. (Outside of the Lord and my kids, my daddy is my strength and I love him in ways words could never express, and I knew as long as the Lord and my daddy was there, I could come out of this thing that was happening to me). The paramedics were asking me what my name was, trying to get me to tell them my social security number or my address. My dad was pleading with them not to take me, but they said that if I didn't tell them any information they would have to take me to the hospital.

My dad began to call out to me and I could feel myself

reaching for my daddy as he took my hands and told me he knew that I could do it, and if I could give them the information that they needed, he would take me with him. He promised he wouldn't leave me. He told me to say my name, social and to tell the paramedics where I was. The spirit in me began to speak out loud. (I know it was the anointing because I couldn't talk) the Holy Ghost spoke right through me and gave them the information they needed in order to release me to my daddy. I remember one of the paramedics saying that I may have been on some drug type of drug; I began to cry out to the Lord to assure them that I didn't use drugs and I wasn't on drugs. I remember them saying that my pupils had dilated so much it was as if I was into another world. The other paramedic had already called the police for back up because they weren't sure what they were running into. When the police got there they began to ask what was going on and started to question my husband. While doing so, the other officer went and ran his name in the computer to find out that he had a warrant for domestic violence on me as well as an injunction.

They took him to jail, and the paramedic released me to my dad. They insisted that he get me check out right away. My stepson called his mom to pick him up and my dad took my kids and me with him. My dad kept the 3 oldest kids and I had to take the two babies, (I had two kids 18 months apart from each other,) because they were being nursed. My sister took me to her house with the kids and I stayed there overnight so that I could get some rest.   I wanted to die; I didn't want to live anymore; I didn't want to hurt anymore; I didn't want to cry anymore; I didn't want my kids to hurt anymore; I didn't' want to be beaten anymore. I just wanted someone to love me genuinely, not love me to death. Still trying to fill that void to a point that some days I would take a drive and want to drive the car off a bridge to kill me and the kids. I was tired, but I didn't want anyone to have to raise my kids. I couldn't do that to them because they deserved better. I couldn't kill myself and leave my kids knowing they needed me, so suicide was not a valid option for me although I wanted to die, thank you Lord. I wanted to die again and again but I had so much to live for!

Chapter 15 - Some of My Safety Zones

Countless times I had to run to my church for my place of safety. Not many people in the church knew what I was going through. Only the people that I was able to cry to, the ones that would worship with me, stay up and cry with me. I have to admit my Pastor Davy was always an ear and a savior. I could call my Pastor in the middle of the night and he would make sure that someone was there to let me into the church (if not himself). My first lady (Sis. Davy) would pray with and for me; Sis. Terrica, Sis. Tracy, Sis. Deon, Sis. Ferguson, Sis. JR, my Mother Gooden and Dea. Tony, were people I could always rely on. I was able to call on any of those prayer warriors and they would pray with me until no end. They let me in the church, and loved me through my pain. Terrica and Tracy would stay with me until I would fall asleep with the kids. They would lock me in the church and leave us there, I awake in the middle of the night and would lay on the alter praying all night. I would fall asleep on the altar and waking up all through the night crying out to God for direction. If I didn't know anything else, I knew how to pray. Some days I didn't call anyone at all because I was so embarrassed and didn't want them to realize how bad it really was (although they knew). Dea. Tony would come in the sanctuary and he tell me to stop praying with my head down to God, that I was beautiful and God wanted to see my face. Dea. Tony always spoke with authority. He told me to lift my head to the sky no matter what was going on around me.

There have been occasions when, I would sleep in my car all weekend with my kids. Some nights we would sleep in the Publix, Kmart, or McFarland Park parking lot, or we would get a hotel. I never understood how we always made it through the night, how we ate, or had some form of shelter, it was only GOD. I see that although I was going through what the enemy thought was going to kill me but God was still there watching over me. I understand I am chosen, and I am a royal priest hood, and the Lord was then allowing me to see that in spite of *Psalms 37:25* *"I'd never seen the righteous forsaken nor his seed begging bread"* my kids and I never once went hungry or had to go around and beg anyone for food. **OH BUT GOD!**

Then there was my sister Cookie; we have had to run to her house and hide for weeks at a time for me to get away from him. She dared him to come to her house. My sister Cookie is a little special ☺ and he didn't want to deal with her too much. I recall him telling my sister that she was forcing me to go out with one of her male friends, and she said "John do you really think she was a virgin when you met her? Then if she wasn't a virgin then how in the hell can I push a grown woman up to sleep with someone else?" She really cursed him out good. I was always able to run to her when I needed but even after that, I didn't let her know how bad it really was. I had to run to Wimauma with my cousin Brenda and stay days at a time but he didn't fool with Brenda either because she would chop him down to size. I always made it seem as if it wasn't that bad. I even fooled myself into thinking that several times, always saying, "It's not that bad, other people have died in this mess and I'm still alive." In all actuality it was that bad, but because I had the hands of God on my life and a called PURPOSE God wasn't going to allow me to die BUT LIVE as HE promised earlier on. I learned that the enemy can ONLY touch you with God's permission BUT he can't kill me and boy he was touching me from every direction, from childhood but this situation was bad, **OH BUT GOD**, wouldn't let that enemy kill me.

My cousin Fuggie, I have had to go to her house a few times as well. He didn't deal with her either because she would have chopped him down to size. He knew not to come to her house, but for the most part he was never sure where I was. Then there was a safe place that I could always run to. This chick would stay up all night and pray for me, cry, talk; whatever I wanted to do she'd do it. I love her so much because she saw some of the really bad parts, both her and her husband. Sabrina and Leon witnessed so much pain within the kids. Some nights when I was too ashamed to call Fuggie, my Pastor, Cookie or anyone else and was too out of it to go to a hotel, I would go all the way out to Valrico, to Leon and Sabrina house. It was times that I would go there in the middle of the night and the kids were exhausted. My oldest daughter being more exhausted than any of the other kids because she helped me haul the kids in and out the car. I was still nursing two babies at the time, and would call Brina in the wee hours of the morning and her and Leon would invite me to come over. Leon was so good to my kids and they love him even today. He would go and get the covers and make sure that the kids were comfortable and Brina would sit and cry with me, pray with me and just literally hurt with me (bring tears to me as I type this part right now because we talk about things all the time. She has been my friend for about 26 years today 4-8-11) and I love her so much, she and Leon have been such an important part of my life in general let alone the abuse. I thank GOD for them for so many nights, all times of night they would open their doors and make us comfortable and hate for us to leave because they didn't know if they would ever see me again. Yet even they don't know how many times I DIDN'T call them.

Brina and I have been together and have rode up on this man while he was actually with another woman. I was pregnant when we followed him and another woman to the hotel. He refused to let me in though, and it was just draining because although I have always been the type to put my good face on, Brina knew me like none other. She saw the pain and hurt in me and little did she know, I saw the pain and hurt in her eyes that she was feeling for me, OH BUT GOD! I was a lucky woman to have the Holy Ghost speaking in tongues. I had a relationship with God. I didn't know that then either, but God knew just what He was doing in my life. We need to realize that God made us from the foundation of the earth and He knows every strain of hair on our heads *(Luke 12:7 Even every hair on your head has been counted. Don't be afraid! You are worth more than many sparrows.)* God has been watching over me through it all.

My relationship with God was my real hiding place the entire time. To God be the glory, and I can't think of all the locations that God gave me as a shield of protection when it was needed. Some days I did wonder what I was going to feed my kid, I would end up working late and having to call my dad or mom to ask if my kids could come there until I got off from work. My mom (bless her heart because God is in charge of that as well), made sure she fed them before I got off and would even have food that she'd say I could eat but I'd act like I didn't want it. Sometimes I would eat it and other time I would be hungry or would've eaten at work (as long as my kids had eaten). Then off we went to find out where we would sleep for that night. Other nights we would go home and see how he was acting, if he's acting fine we'd stay home, but if he was acting on edge, we would figure out a way to escape so that he didn't start beating on me. My oldest daughter knew the routine; we would act like we were running bath water, but I would put the kids out the window. I would tell them to run to the end of the street until I got away from him to jump in the car and pick them up down the street. Even then God was watching over my oldest daughter at night standing on the corner with the other kids. There was never any police coming to take them from me, and nothing ever happened to them in the midst of all of this drama. You must remember, my daughter had the Holy Ghost too she was a praying young girl. Now I understand why God allowed her to receive the Holy Ghost at the young age of eight years old. He knew that she and mommy would need to go into warfare together, a lot of days we'd be parked in a parking lot praying like never before over the other kids until she drifted off to sleep. I'm glad I had a praying doctor that I could confide in; we've had to run to her house for days just to get away and she'd pray for us. She even tried to minister to my husband, tried to show him where God has plans for his life and can use him, but that only worked for so long. We even got under the wings of Pastor Gomez and his wife and they really ministered to us for a long time and it seemed to work for a minute as well, but never lasting long, he begin to do the same things, he didn't want to hear what was being said, he wanted his drugs, woman and the abuse.

Chapter 16 - Some of the Physical Abuse Stopped, but Then

As time went on, I had gotten fed up and the kids where drained too. We got to the point that, when he wasn't home by a certain time, we would leave the house to go stay with someone else; sleep in the park, apartment complex or anywhere. It was almost like we knew his schedule. Sometimes I'd set the alarm to leave at 5 or 6am because he would be coming home any time after 6am. I'd take the kids to places like the flea market or the airport to watch the planes (before 911); we would stay gone until we felt he had slept all of his high off. I often think about how we used to have our school, work and church clothes in the trunk so that we could just go where we needed to go if we were on the run, that bag never left the trunk, sleeping gear and all.

One day I was in the kitchen cooking and my husband was cleaning and had the kids cleaning as well. He was yelling and screaming at them because they weren't moving like he felt they should. He was mainly yelling at my oldest daughter, and he'd always tell her she was smart mouthed just like her mother but she really wasn't. He continued to yell and I kept doing what I was doing, and then all of a sudden, I heard my daughter yell, and I went running to find out what had happened. I found out that he had slapped her and said her mouth was too smart. I asked him why he had did that, and he said that she talked back to him. He was high at that time and my daughter was crying and went in to take a shower. I followed her into the bathroom to find out from her, and when she pulled the shower curtain back, I saw her face and I lost it. I ran into the room and asked him why, I wanted to kill him, and he said he had not really done anything. I said to him "You slapped my baby, are you crazy, you left your hand print in her face!" He then begin to cry and say he was sorry **HE APOLOGIZED**, and that he didn't mean to hit her but she got smart at the mouth and she reminded him of me. I walked away and went back into the bathroom with my daughter and asked her what she wanted me to do about it. I know some are saying I'm crazy but at that time I was, I was lost and out of my own control. My daughter said nothing, but I'm assuming that was because she didn't want to start any more problems. My baby was crushed because he'd never hit her and to do that just shocked her. When she got out the shower he cried and apologized but I saw me in her, she grit her teeth and said it was ok and kept it moving, but it wasn't ok. My mind was going 100 miles per hour because I was thinking if he so quickly felt like she was me and hit her, when will he do it again or when will he try to touch her because now I knew his mind was really warped this dude done hit my child. The next morning when he left I called our doctor and told her I needed to see her and we went to her and she saw my daughters face. She said that I could press charges but I would probably go to jail or get the kids taken from me because he had a history of abuse on me, and he had an injunction but I still had him around and it could all fall back on me. I was afraid, and I didn't want DCF to come in and take my kids.   Although my daughter face went down in a couple of days she couldn't go to school until it was better. She still has a dark scar under her eye where he hit her and her self-esteem is so jarred because of that scar under her eye even to this very day. Many women say that these men aren't hitting your kids, but if they aren't now, just keep them around and eventually they will. Although he never hit her again or any of them for that matter, I still watched him carefully around her because he was seeing her as me and I was afraid. Thank God he never tried to touch her.

Chapter 17 – I think I'm Numb Now

I was tired now and truly ready to get out, all the threats, all the abuse, all of it, I was tired and didn't care anymore, I had become numb, yet I was unsure how I'd make it without being torn down (funny right) although he didn't pay bills, handle any business and/or family important issues, and couldn't keep a job, I still didn't know how I would function without him that control. I had become content with being called bitches, whores, ugly, unattractive, filthy, and dirty. I was used to being told that no man will ever want me for me, and he would just want to use me. He told me no man would want me with 5 kids. He used to tell me that I didn't have anything to offer any man but sex. So many times he would carry on about how other women were much better than me. I got to where my heart began to turn into steel and could barely feel his words penetrate me anymore. The funny thing is, sometimes I would actually fight him back now and although I couldn't physically beat him, especially while he was on drugs, I got to the point where I was just tired of him beating me, I wanted to die anyways, so just kill me why don't you. I began to learn certain techniques and started to realize that he'd always try to hit me with his first blow as hard as he could and break me down. I learned not get so close to him, and if I was already trapped and couldn't get away, I knew if he was back too far, he couldn't hit me like he wanted to. I would keep my distance from him to shake his balance, and a few times I got away because I pulled a gun on him, but I couldn't pull the trigger because the gun was illegal. There were no laws for women for killing an abusive husband at the time and I couldn't leave my babies like that, there are many women sitting in prison for shooting (not even killing them bastards) abusive men. He didn't know my mind-set, so he'd back off.

When he was high he'd still charge at me and we fought over the gun one night but every since that night I through that gun out because I fired it at him but thank God I missed, but I began to keep things at arm reach so that I can pepper spray him long enough for the kids and me to get away, or keep things that I can hit him with to get away, I taught my kids (especially my oldest daughter) so many different ways to get always until it was sickening, but they knew the escape routine. I got to the point that I would fight him long enough to get the kids out the door and into the car; I kept a personal cell phone in my daughter's room under her bed, for her to call 911 when she heard something wrong in the middle of the night. So many nights my oldest daughter went to bed with knives and screw drivers under her pillow for fear she'd have to hurt him if he came in on me and I couldn't get him off or if he came to ever harm her or her siblings.

My oldest daughter had to grow up fast because of that life, and I began to build up hatred within myself and I wanted him dead, I sometime felt like I could have turned into an abuser, I started calling him names and saying things to hurt him as well, I wanted him to feel what I felt, but at that time I didn't realize what was slowly being created within me {if a victim is not careful, they can turn into an abuser, rather it be towards themselves, the kids, the husband or other people) and sometimes they die with that hatred and bitterness within them and the only person that could bring it out and heal them is the Lord. Being a woman of God, I had the upper hand on hearing of the Spirit, although sometime I ignored the spirit of the Lord because the wounds/hurt was so deep within me, but the Lord ministered to me and allowed me to know that I was becoming an abuser in many ways, although it wasn't against my kids, it was towards my abuser, I still was a woman of God and I had to continue to pray for him. {If you aren't save, you won't understand that right now} but I had to continue to be strong in the Lord. It wasn't easy for me at all because I didn't want to pray for him, but I had to find a way.

My oldest daughter tried for so long to pray for him but it was so hard for her, she loved him because he was daddy (actually her step-dad) but she had a hate down in her that up to this day

6/20/2003 and it hasn't left her as I edit and prepare to publish this book (7-22-11) she still has bitterness in her and fighting within to make it stop but so many memories still haunt her today. Edited 3/14/2014 she's finally forgiven him.

Chapter 18 – Finally It's Done

I was finally tired and my church was having revival all week, the kids and I attended every night and I sung in the choir and the Spirit of God told me I needed to be there because the Anointing was high and something was about to happen but I didn't know what it was, I just felt it all in my spirit.

The final night of revival, the kids and I got home and I was singing and praising God, my husband was in the house and for some reason he felt the need to argue. I continue to sing and praise God, although my flesh was starting to buckle, I continued to praise. He blocked me in the living room, (I could see my oldest daughter peeking from the kitchen) I told him I didn't want to argue and that I was too high in the anointing to argue so please just stop it, he continued but I still had my car keys in my hands. He went into a rage and acted as if he was going to hit me, when he swung he missed and I almost emptied the can of mace that was attached to my key ring into his eyes; he begin to scream and hold his face and I ran out the door to call the police. By the time the police got there, he was gone (as always) but I'm sure he was hurting. As I walked into the door, I saw that my daughter was on the floor shaking and screaming, I thought that she was just acting out of finally being tired like I was, little did I know my baby was having a mild break-down, so the police called the paramedics. When they arrived, they put my daughter in the back and calmed her down, they told me that she had a mild break-down and I needed to get her seen, but I refuse to let them take her and told them that I would do it. (I was afraid that DCF would step in and take them from me). They stayed with us until she was stable and we went into the house, I sat inside of one of the living rooms (I had a house with 3 living rooms) as I walked up the hall, she met me and said to me "momma, daddy is going to kill you, your are going to die from daddy", I said to her "no baby, I won't die, he is gone this time and won't be back", my baby turn to walk away and said "you say that all the time but daddy gone kill you". She's said that to me before and she was right, I had said he wasn't coming back many of times and let him back every time, but it was something about that night, that I meant it and was going to stand on it and I did.

He kept trying to call and come back but I would not give in this time, he threaten to kill me but I was ready to die, I was tired after watching my baby on that floor screaming, reminding me of myself that night I had the break-down. It was rough on us for a while because he would hide outside the house and when we would open the door, he would jump from behind the bushes and come in the house and hold us there with the gun until he came down off his high, of course I was doing my same sexual favors to bring him down while in my head planning to get away for good. When he would leave the house, I would lock him out and I got an alarm, but we still had to be careful when we left the house. When we left out in the morning time for school and works, I had to hold the youngest baby and the middle child, while my oldest held the other baby and we had to run out the door into the car (that was parked right against the door) and immediately lock the doors so he would not jump into the car, as he had numerous of times before. We had to come home at different times, and would circle the house numerous times before going in, so he wouldn't run into the house behind us. One particular day he grabbed a hold to the car window as I was driving, while trying to punch me in my face through the window; as he held to the top of the car; I went around the block driving fast trying to throw him off about 5 times. (The kids screaming and yelling asking daddy to get off the car) Finally I told the kids to put on their seat belts and prepared to flip the car over just to get him off, I went at a high rate of speed (as the neighbors watched and called the police), I hit the speed bump and the corner so fast until he flew off the car into the neighbor's yard, he was so high, he hit the ground and jumped up and begin to chase the car. As always, by the time the police got there, he was gone. I found out later he had a broken finger but that still didn't stop him from bothering me.

Finally I got tired of the running from the house, he would call and threaten to come to the house and kill me and the kids (he had started threatening the kids and my dad, saying he was going to hurt what was dear to my heart). I would stay awake all night watching over my kids, looking out the window and praying. That life was just as worst to me than it was to stay with him and fight because it was scarier not knowing where he was than to just know he was right there (that is also why I let him come back so many times) but I know he was going to kill me this time and I heard something different in my daughters voice when she told me that that particular night.

Chapter 19 – I'm Ready to Die

I went and got $100,000.00 of insurance on myself and double if I die by accident, because he would try to drive me off the road whenever he had a car and saw me. I called my cousin Brenda and asked if anything happened to me, if she would take my kids and she promised me that she would and take good care of them. Now I was ready to die being as my kids would be taken care of. I had gone to the funeral home, sat down with the funeral director and told him everything that I wanted in order to make sure that no one spent the wrong way for my funeral and to make sure my kids would have something to live off of and no one would ever say they had to financially take care of them.

He called one night and said that he was coming over, kick the front door in, and kill me and the kids. I begged him to come and told him I was unlocking the door and I would be sitting in the living room waiting on him because I was no longer afraid to die. I assured him that he needed to be ready because I wasn't just going to lay down and die, he would have to fight and if it was by his bare hands it wasn't going to happen so easy because I was now tired. I got on the phone, called my spiritual mother and told her how much I loved her and that I may die and it was alright. I told her that I was ready, and she pleaded with me to leave the house, but I told her I wasn't going to move.

I said that I was tired and that I wanted to end the mess and hung up the phone.

I fell to my knees and called on Jesus to inform HIM that I may be on my way but it was alright, and I needed him to make sure my kids would be watched over because I was ready to die. I was exhausted, and waited up all night, he never showed. I called him back and asked what was taking so long, and he said that I was crazy and hung up on me. That morning I opened the front door with no fear and put my kids in the car and locked them in while I locked up the house. I wasn't afraid anymore. As we are driving down the streets, he drove up behind us speeding and driving crazy trying to run me off the road. I called the police as we were driving in hopes to drive him right into the police. They were directing me to an area where they would be, but by the time I got to the area, my husband had turned off, but not before I doubled around and got the tag number off the car he was driving and gave it to the officers. He would watch me at work every day and tell me what I wore and when I went to lunch, he would follow me on the ride home and try to run me off the interstate but for everything he did, I reported it, now it was time to move on by any means necessary.

Chapter 20 - Injunction and Divorce

Finally I got strong enough to go through with the divorce, after I had been through Bay Area Legal two times before. Bay Area Legal was the light at the end of my tunnel. They never once turned me down. They walked me through this ordeal even when I was afraid and wanted to give in on the divorce. (You may ask why I wanted to give up on the divorce. I didn't know if I could function without his control over my life and I was afraid he would find me and kill me, most women are killed after the injunction and divorce) I went forward with the divorce, the attorney that I had was very nice and he gave me a voice, when I say he gave me a voice, he asked me what I wanted from my divorce. I was so used to being controlled I wasn't sure what I wanted, I asked him "what should I do" and he told me that this was now time for me to get my voice back, he was there to do what I needed him to do for me, I told him, I just want him to stay away from me and my kids, I want to be divorced from him but he will still find me because I still had his last name, he let me know that I didn't have to keep his last name, I could return to my maiden name and that was my request.

They tried to serve my husband and it was so hard because he never stayed still. He did come to my house one morning and

I let him in and told him I would be back. When I left him at the house I called my attorney to get him served for the divorce and they served him, but by the time the police got there to get him on the warrants he was gone. He continued to harass me on my job so I called the police and the sheriff's department came out. It was a female detective that took the report and I told her the history between the abuse and she took it personal. She would come by and check on me at work every now and then, she gave me her direct line and told me to make sure I contacted her every time he contacted me because she was going to issue warrants for everything he did and we did just that. I was coming back from lunch one day and he was up the street watching for me. This time, he didn't see me when I came back through because his head was turned. I went by fast enough to call the detective and she came out, as she prepared to catch him, he saw her and tried to flee in the car to his mother's house, jumped out the car and jump the fence but the Detective jumped the fence with him and pulled her gun. They finally caught him, thank you Jesus!

When it was time to go to court for the injunction, I was afraid to face him but my attorney told me not to let him intimidate me because he was in jail and couldn't get to me and wasn't getting out any time soon. I prepared myself to walk into the court room to deal with the injunction. The Judge was so furious with his behavior, to see he had been arrested 28 times for me alone, had violated 4 injunctions, the Judge honored me a 25 year injunction keeping him away from the kids and me (good till 2015). Months later the divorce came through and I was divorce March of 2001 from my monster and he was sentenced to prison for six years. Today I know it really was "MY" Lord and Savior because he is using me now to tell somebody this story as I sit on the Board of Directors for Bay Area Legal where I was a victim and now I'm a Board Member – the light and the end of my tunnel. It took me a while to start learning my way back, I was still wrapped into the church, and I lived at the church so much, my kids was starting to lack things, I say that because I didn't balance time with them after all we had been through and I was pleasing people more than anything. I moved to Valrico and was about to start my life over for my kids and I. I was very vulnerable and wasn't sure which way to turn, I do know that a man was the last thing on my mind. I just wanted my kids and God that was enough for me!

To be continued

Silent Scream Series Part 3 Are you serious, it's not over yet? The final installment of the Silent Scream Series titled *"Someone Took Advantage of My Vulnerability"* will be released soon in conjunction with the book titled *"The Silent Screams of a Child"* by Yolanda's daughter Johnna Lee. You will be able to read first-hand how not only did Yolanda go through it, but so did her daughter, it will be a short story but it will be a testimony within itself... You will experience for the first time, how a mother and child can have the same silent screams at the same time, giving way to the beginnings of the cycle of abuse. This will take you places that you may have never even knew existed unless you've walked it. **Except: "Someone Took Advantage of my Vulnerability" Part III**.......*When she finally let it out that he'd been touching her and that she was afraid that he was going to go further, I lost it. Now here I am again, with the shame on my face, back at Bay Area Legal Services trying to get another divorce because this man touched my daughter and I started to blow his brains out, but thanks to my Pastor, I didn't kill that man and today I'm glad I didn't. What a life I've lived, I'm so tired; I just want someone to love me and I still waiting on God to send that special someone into my life even now!*

Except: *"The Silent Screams of a Child" by Johnna Lee*

- - - - - -****** - - - - - -****** - - - - - -******

Growing up for me was everything but normal, I saw and heard a lot of things that my little eyes and ears should not have. My mother met my step-father (the monster) when I had just turned 3 years old. He made our lives a living hell. It wasn't that bad at first because he had many faces (that we didn't realize). He was so nice to us, especially to me and I enjoyed him coming around when he did (normally my mom didn't bring men around me). He would sometimes put me on the handle bars of his bicycle and take me for rides to the store and would always buy my favorite snacks (pickle, sour cream and cheddar potato chips with the French onion dip, we would come back, get in front of the television and just eat them all up, just the two of us. I was already spoiled by my mom, but when he came around I was very spoiled. Time went on and he just showed me so much love and he bought his son around and I felt like that was another brother to me. In due time, hearing his son call him daddy, I started calling him daddy as well, my mom didn't like it at first but she became OK with it because he was alright with it. We had slowly become like a family so why not.

With all the love he was showing to us, at first I didn't realize that my mom was pretending to smile some days (she's a good pretender, smiling on the outside while dying on the inside). Slowly the silent screams within my moms' face began to show more, I begin to hear yelling from my dad but I didn't pay it a lot of attention because my dad was nice to me and wasn't yelling at me. As time went on I did start to pay attention that he was slowly changing towards my mom with the yelling, wanting to know her every move, always thinking she was up to something, wanting her to stay in the house and only be with him. They would argue now all the time (if she went somewhere or did something without talking to him first). I would hear my mom cry (she didn't know I could hear her) she wasn't the crying type she was happy with just my oldest brother and me (although my oldest brother stayed with my grandparents all the time). Although I was a little kid, I still knew something wasn't right between them.

Over the weeks, months, years, his yelling turned into beatings, I was always scared and nervous when he was around, he had begun to wear so many faces, I didn't know who was who with him (although he was still nice to me) I hated how he was treating my mom; at that time, I just wanted him to go. I remember so many times the police had started coming out to our house but my dad would be gone by the time they got there. I recall sleeping in the shed outside our house because we were hiding from my dad and my mom didn't want to fight in front of me anymore, she was tired. I use to see roaches and rats in the shed and was so glad when Ms. Patrice got home to let us get in her back door or her back window. I recall sleeping in the parks in the stroller my mom use to have me in, because he would have taken my mom car and we had to get away before he got there, so she would put me in the stroller and we would walk. It would be so dark but my mom didn't care as long as she kept me safe and she was safe from my daddy (the monster).

My mom got pregnant from him and I knew he would be around forever now. By now I've completely lost my childhood, I couldn't play out in the yard anymore, I couldn't roll the ball and do kid things anymore because we was running so much. I used to go to my grandma house a lot (on my biological dad side), but I didn't want to go anymore because I wanted to be with my mom, I didn't like the way she was being treated and wanted to be there for her if she needed me. I say needed me because I noticed that after he would yell and I would hear a lot of movement (that my mom thought I didn't hear by putting me in the other room), I knew he was fighting my mom and was scared he would hurt her. When he left I would go lay in the bed with my mom, my mom and I would bake cookies and do so much together but I saw she was tired in the face, she wasn't the mommy that I was used to, he was hurting my mom even while she was pregnant.

As time went on I recall so many incidents (but I'll just touch on a couple of hard memorable ones). As I got older I began to realize he only act like this when he used the drugs and alcohol (I would hear my mom beg him to stop using the drugs and I would hear him cry after the fact of beating her and blame it on the drugs and alcohol). Sometimes he would come in the house yelling "where he at, where he at," walking fast and going through the house looking under the bed, in the freezer, cabinets, all through the house and my mom would grab us and put us in the room with her in order for us not to see this, but it was too late, this was so surreal to me, this is something you see on television and laugh because it can't be true, a person can't just hallucinate for real, well it was real. He always felt like my mom was seeing someone else other than him. I hated that he used drugs because when he was sober, he was the best daddy in the world; he was like my personal daddy (outside of my own biological father). I used to always hear my mom praying (especially when he wasn't home) she has always been a praying woman in spite of whatever she was doing in her life (good or bad), so that taught me to pray because she prayed with me as well. There are so many times I felt my mom should stop praying because God didn't listen to her anyway, I felt that because most of the time when she got off her knees from praying, he would still come in the door and start yelling about the next man and my mom always tried to put on that smile so that I wouldn't worry and she'd try to calm him down in front of me and tell me to go in my room and play for a little while, but I didn't want to go (although I didn't say that to my mom I wasn't a disrespectful kid). I would go in the room and listen. He would jump on my mom sometimes he would beat her so bad, he would kick her and everything till she couldn't see out of her eyes but she still cooked, cleaned and all, while trying to hide her face from me, but I saw it and pretended not to because I loved my mom. When he would leave, I'd get in the bed with her and take care of her, but hear her cries in the middle of the night. I was no longer a child anymore. I used to watch my mom cook, she would show me how to cook certain things, especially spaghetti and I'd watch how she cleaned the house. I was learning so much good from my mom. Well watching her paid off because sometimes he would beat her so bad she could barely move and she'd taught me how to get my chair, put it up the sink and to the stove and she taught me how to do what I needed to do as a little lady. My mom was also sick a lot from her migraine and sickle cell that would flare up, she would be in pain from all of that but she still kept moving, refuse to go the hospital and she stayed strong with me right by her side. I cooked my spaghetti, fixed the plates for all of us, helped take care of my little sister, cleaned up and we'd get in the bed with my mom praying that the monster would not come home. (I wanted to be and was the best helper my mom had, because we didn't take our business outside of our house).

Every time he would fight her, he'd sometimes cry more than her, then he'd promise to never do it again, but I quickly learned he wasn't telling the truth. He would sometimes disappear for a few days after he beat her real bad and go stay with his other girlfriends that he had. When he did come home and start the yelling and screaming, I would always grab my baby sister and take her in the room, sometimes I'd put my hands over her ears or turn the televisions up real loud so she wouldn't hear my mom muffled screams when he started beating and kicking on her. I wanted to come out the room and kill him because I was tired. My mom tried to muffle her cries, tried not to yell with him, tried to calm him down by telling him we could hear him and to please stop the yelling, please calm down. I would hear him raping my mom (when she didn't think I heard it) forcing her to do things she would tell him she didn't want to do as the anger well up in my little soul. I felt one day he was going to kill my mom and what would we do, all we had was our mom.

One day it began to get out of hand, he was yelling like crazy so loud in a different way than normal and I was very scared, I didn't know what was going to happen! I grabbed my little sister and went in the room and began to pray. The argument lead into the hallway (between all the bedrooms) I was peeking around the corner to see what was going on and to my eyes was a shock, I saw my dad reach up at my mom, grab her head and slam it into the wall, knocking a hole into the wall, my little sister ran to my side to see what was going on as we watch my mom slide to the floor and didn't move, I just knew she was dead. I ran to my mom side to see if she was dead, her eyes were rolled back into her head and I was screaming and crying, my little sister came and got on the side of me, unsure what was going on but she knew it was bad, she looked like I looked back then at her age when it first started.

My dad began to cry, he got a wet rag and I sat there and rubbed my mom head as I looked down at her telling her how much I loved her, finally she begin to open her eyes and she looked up at me for a brief second, we got her up and into her bed; my little sister and I got in the bed with my mom and we laid there with her all day as I took care of her and my little sister (making sure my little sister was fed). My dad cried (as always) and he left for a day or so.

We loved our mom so much (and still do). I began to hate this man I used to love and call my daddy, the man that took me on bicycle rides to get snacks, he was now a monster to me, he was someone I wish God would take away from us and never give back. I wanted my mommy back.

I could go on and on but I'll stop here, there is so much more from the **"Silent Screams of the Little Girl."** Stay tuned and be watchful, I'll be coming out one day in the near future. I say to anyone that is in a domestic violence (any violence); please get out, if not for yourself, for the kids. You don't realize what you are doing to your children in the mess. I'm just grateful to God that my mom got us out safe, she is alive and well and thank God for Bay Area Legal Services for all of their support in getting my mom the divorce.

Stay tuned and be blessed! **By: Johnna Nytajah Lee**

To be continued...

Resource Page

The Spring of Tampa Bay
813-247-7233
www.thespring.org

Hillsborough County Lawyer Referral
(813) 221-7780

Crisis Center
813-234-1234

Abuse Hotline
1-800-962-2873

Tampa Police Department
813-276-3200

Plant City Police Department
813-757-9200

Temple Terrace Police Department
813-989-7111

Hillsborough County Sheriff's Office
813-247-8000 www.hcso.tampa.fl.us

Victims Information and Notification Information
800-398-3150

Injunction Office813-276-8100

Resource Page

Victim Compensation800-226-6666
Florida Dept. of Corrections
www.dc.state.fl.us

Florida Government Offices
www.myflorida.com
State Attorney - 813-272-5400
13th Judicial Circuit
700 E. Twiggs Street Room 711Tampa, FL
33602www.SAO13th.com

Someone Almost Loved Me to Death

www.bethanysgroup.com